RICO WILSON

SUCCESS FOR LOSERS

EPROGRAM YOURSELF FOR AN INCREDIBLE LIFE

TATE PUBLISHING
AND **ENTERPRISES,** LLC

Published by Tate Publishing & Enterprises, LLC
127 E. Trade Center Terrace | Mustang, Oklahoma 73064 USA
1.888.361.9473 | www.tatepublishing.com

Tate Publishing is committed to excellence in the publishing industry. The company reflects the philosophy established by the founders, based on Psalm 68:11,
"The Lord gave the word and great was the company of those who published it."

Book design copyright © 2012 by Tate Publishing, LLC. All rights reserved.
Cover design by Kenna Davis
Interior design by Nathan Harmony

Published in the United States of America

ISBN: 978-1-61862-075-0
1. Self-Help / Personal Growth / Success
2. Self-Help / General
12.01.23

Dedication

To my beautiful wife, Valerie, who makes me deliriously happy and inspires me to succeed.

Table of Contents

Introduction

Do you ever feel like there is a dark cloud above your head that follows you around wherever you go? Do you ever feel like God or the universe, or whatever you believe in, has singled you out for failure and has decided to make sure that you can't succeed—no matter what you do?

Do you ever get angry with God for "not allowing" you to be successful? Can you look back and see a pattern of consistently *not* getting what you want out of life? Do you feel like you can and should be more successful, but you just keep missing it for some reason that you can't quite identify?

Do you sometimes feel like there just has to be some hidden secret to becoming successful and that you will never be successful until you find out exactly what that secret is?

Do you ever feel envious or frustrated because it seems like others around you have become successful fairly easily, and it has not happened for you—even with more effort? Does it feel like you're running a race, and you're the only one dragging heavy weights behind you?

If you answered yes to any of these questions, you need this book and you need it *now*. The fact is, there *is* a secret to being successful, and if you answered yes to any of the questions above, then you are probably not one of the lucky ones who inherited the "success gene" naturally—which means that you do need to learn this secret somehow, or you are probably doomed to continue living in frustration and dissatisfaction until you do.

Some people have *it* naturally, without even knowing what *it* is—or even that *it* exists; they don't need to learn it. It appears that you, my friend, do not. You must learn the ideas in this book if you want to change your life and become a success. That doesn't mean you can't become as successful as someone who has *it* naturally—you may even become more successful—but not until you learn the principles contained in this book.

Because this book is called *Success for Losers* and I just told you that you need it desperately, you may be tempted to feel insulted because it sounds like I'm calling you a loser. Well, before you get too mad, it's up to you to make that determination—not me. And let me define *loser* for the purpose of our training here. I'm probably using this word a little differently than you're used to thinking of it.

Most people think of a *loser* as someone they don't want to be around, because of some set of obnoxious or annoying, unattractive traits. But I'm going to use this word very literally and objectively. You're either winning in life or you're losing. Sometimes there's some of both happening at the same time, but the real question is: Are you really getting everything you want out of life?

For our purposes here, we can say that a winner is someone who wins most of the time, and a loser is someone who loses most of the time. This does not mean, again for our purposes, that a loser is some weird, creepy guy who can't do anything right. It's just the objective results that we're looking at here.

To elaborate a little, I'm going to define a loser as someone who has consistently *not* gotten the long-term results they want out of life; who wishes they could be, do, and have more but doesn't know how; or who is consistently dissatisfied with life for whatever reason.

I'll say that a winner is someone who is happy and excited about life, who consistently gets what they want out of life, who has the confidence to go out and make something happen, and who isn't plagued by "bad luck" or a long-term series of unfortunate events. A winner is someone whose actions and responses consistently put them on the winning side of whatever situation comes along. This is someone who is confident, positive, and bounces back quickly if something does go wrong. Someone who chooses what they want to be, do, and have in life and makes it happen.

That's a winner. If this does not describe you, then for purposes of this book—you may consider yourself a loser. Only up to this point, of course. This can change right now. But you need to know where you're starting and where you want to go in order to figure out how you're going to get there. If you really want to go from loser to winner as quickly as possible, learn and implement the contents of this book. If you do what this book will teach you to do, you will become a winner and shake off those losing qualities forever.

Of course, I realize that we could choose to define a middle area between winner and loser. And I'm not suggesting that if things aren't perfect in your life you should give up or walk around feeling bad about yourself. But I am strongly suggesting that for our purposes here, if you're not firmly in the winner category, you can definitely benefit from this book. If your life isn't everything you want it to be, let's change that starting right now.

Allow me to introduce myself. My name is Rico, and I used to be a loser. Don't get me wrong; I never thought of myself as a loser either. I was good at everything—usually among the best at whatever I chose to do. Everything came easily to me. I could do whatever I wanted to do. I'm talented and ambitious; I communicate and present myself well. I'm intelligent and have a decent education, by most standards, and in some things I'm actually considered to be an expert.

The problems I had didn't have to do with not being able to do something. It wasn't a social problem, like being awkward or unattractive or anything like that. It wasn't that I couldn't learn to do something well. In fact, I could learn to do anything well. I proved that by the gigantic number of things that I learned to do well.

No, my problem was that, in spite of my great potential and a variety of useful qualities, there seemed to be an invisible force that made sure nothing ever worked out for me long term. Sure, things started out great, but long term, nothing ever really worked out just right.

No matter how hard I tried, no matter how hard I worked, no matter how much effort and dedication and persistence I devoted to something, there was always something sabotaging my long-term success. Was it a curse? Did I offend God so irreparably that He simply didn't love me anymore? Was I so dreadfully sinful that I actually deserved a life of frustration and regret?

I always thought I was a good person. I was honest and never tried to hurt anyone. I was devoted to my faith and have even made some very significant sacrifices to do what I thought was right. Sure, I'm far from perfect. I'm not suggesting that I float up out of bed and hit the ceiling in my sleep every night or that I walk around with a halo over my head, but I did consider myself to be one of the "good people."

And I'm not trying to brag about my abilities, by the way. My only purpose in pointing out any of my positive qualities is to show you that there really was a problem and that this problem has nothing to do with a person's ability or potential to succeed. I'm trying to illustrate that a person can have all the ability in the world and still be a "loser" by our definition.

It's not like I failed in life because I simply wasn't capable of success. If that were the case, failure would have made more sense to me. But if someone with lots of ability and drive consistently fails in life, something is wrong. I'm actually quite embarrassed to admit all of this. I never considered myself to be a loser. But results are results.

In spite of having all the ability I could ever need, I still couldn't manage to succeed in life. I tried a million things and always wound up looking for greener grass. And every time I swore up and down that I was going to make something work "this time," something seemingly out of my control prevented my short-term success from becoming long-term success, and I decided that I'd better go try something else—*again*.

So, what was my problem? Why did I spend so much time and effort spinning my wheels just to wind up in my forties with nothing to show for all my sacrifice and hard work?

Well, that's why I wrote this book. After I found out what happened to me and learned how to repair that damage, I realized that there are others out there with the ability and ambition—but who have not gotten the results that even someone with less ability or ambition should reasonably expect to achieve with a reasonable amount of effort.

So, here are the two big questions: Why could I not make my life work, no matter how hard I tried? And more importantly, how could I trade that pattern in for a more successful one?

In the pages that follow, I believe I will answer these questions and others related to it. I wish that someone else had written this book about twenty-five years ago and given me a copy. Maybe I could have saved myself a lot of heartache, pain, overwhelming frustration, hair loss, depression, health problems, financial difficulties, and years of regret.

If you read this introduction and can relate to my situation even a little bit, do yourself a favor and read this book. It may cost you a few bucks, but it cost me a whole lot more.

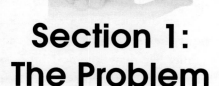

Section 1:
The Problem

So, how is it that someone with all the talent and ability necessary to become highly successful can struggle for years and years without having anything to show for it? Is it lack of focus? Bad timing? Poor decision-making? Impatience?

Yes, it was—all of the above. But beyond that, even though I tried to combat all of those things, it really did seem like some invisible force would come along and ruin everything.

This invisible force would let me start out just fine. It would let me learn how to do what I set out to do. Then it would even let me get off to a good start. But then something would happen. Market conditions, the economy, some personal situation, some frustration or dissatisfaction, or maybe another opportunity came along that looked better to me than what I was doing at the time. It was always something.

My point is that it went far beyond just some trait or set of traits that seemed to sabotage my long-term success. It really did seem like there was an invisible force that would not allow me to be successful, no matter what I did. Even when I accepted that I had made some poor choices or didn't stick something out long enough in the past or something like that—the next time, the problem was something entirely different, such that I could not correct the problem by trying to learn my lesson from the previous incident.

So, what causes this losing phenomenon? Why did I have a problem becoming successful in life in spite of apparently having all the tools I needed? After years of watching this pattern repeat itself, I had to learn what was behind it. If, no matter how hard I tried, the result was always the same, how could I change that result? I had to learn what caused this. And evidently, nothing was going to change until I did.

So, I studied a lot of different things over many years: religion, a little philosophy, motivation, hypnosis, neuro-linguistic programming, sales training, success programming, anything about how the mind works, the law of attraction, quantum physics, meditation, and positive thinking. Anything that looked like it had useful information for me—I wanted to know about it.

Of course, there were things that I noticed were starting to lead down a path I didn't want to go down, so I changed direction. And I learned things that just didn't work, some things I couldn't believe in, things with limited effectiveness, and things that when combined correctly seem to hit the nail right on the head. I now believe that I can accurately explain what caused my problem and how to fix it.

I am, of course, going to incorporate information I learned from some of these sources into what I teach in this book. There may be things in those books or elements of those teachings and philosophies that I disagree with. But there may also be valuable information that I used in drawing my conclusions.

Being a Christian, I have included some biblical references in this book that I find to be very useful. Whatever your belief system is, this book can help anyone who sincerely wants to learn how to go from loser to winner as quickly as possible. If you will learn and use the information contained in this book, you will experience the radical change you've been hoping for.

I studied a lot of different things over the years to finally learn what went wrong with me and how to reprogram myself for success. Some things I could believe in and some things I could not. Some things did not warrant investigation because they were obviously incompatible with my set of accepted truth. For example, as a Christian, I was not going to look into witchcraft in any form.

However, I did find some truth in other things that many readers may not accept—or at least not until they learn a little more about them. For example, I studied hypnosis and some of its related sub-fields. Although I do not believe in past-life regression, for example—because it is incompatible with my set of higher priority beliefs—I do believe that God created our brains to function in a certain way and that it is important to understand how they work so that we can use them properly in order to improve our lives.

Whether you choose to believe in hypnosis or not is up to you. This book does not require the use of hypnosis to be effective. In fact, this book is actually about alternative means to reprogramming your subconscious mind for success—things that you can do on your own, without having to consult a hypnotherapist. There are other ways to correct bad subconscious programming, and we will talk about some of those in this book.

My point is that I found a lot of information out there that is very useful and that doesn't necessarily conflict with other beliefs that are important to me. I have utilized that information and have indeed found it to be accurate, to work, and to still leave me with a belief system that is acceptable to me.

Getting to this point took a while. I studied so many things that I couldn't list them all here if I tried. And I tried all the typical and many not-so-typical things. I tried the traditional positive thinking approach; I broke spiritual curses in intensive Christian curse-breaking workshops; I practiced "spiritual warfare"—some very unique, esoteric stuff I learned from an unlikely source; I used affirmations ad nauseum; I worked on building and exercising faith using a different method from another source; I studied and prayed for hours per day—nothing. I tried large numbers of programs from a wide variety of sources; I read books, listened to tapes, CDs, etc. I tried everything I could accept as a possibility. Sadly, the situation was still not resolved.

Don't get me wrong; when I said "nothing" above, I didn't really mean to say that there was no value in any of the above. Some of these things can have substantial value. But I didn't see the dramatic and quantifiable changes in my life that I was hoping for. The same set of problems still plagued me and followed me everywhere I went.

Perhaps all the things I had been doing all that time helped me to endure my trials better than I would have otherwise. Maybe they served an important purpose in developing my inner strength, perseverance, mettle, or whatever. But what I was really looking for was measurable and substantial success in my life.

Just as I don't want to imply that there was no value in the activities I engaged in above, I also don't want to imply that just because I did not find exactly what I was looking for—at least not right away—that doesn't mean that my beliefs were invalid; nor does it mean that I was not progressing along the certain track that was, perhaps, where I was supposed to be that time, at least making progress in some ways.

But the bottom line is that after making valiant attempts at a number of things that other people swore by or experts endorsed or reputable, successful people taught—I still had not become what I would call "successful."

Fortunately, after years of hard work and study, I did finally stumble across the missing pieces of the puzzle and was able to figure out what went wrong and how to make it right. And since then, my life has dramatically turned around. Now, more things go right instead of wrong. I'm happier than I've ever been, and my health has improved dramatically. In fact, it appears that everything in my life is consistently heading in the right direction. And I'm just getting warmed up.

If you would like to turn your life around and experience the same positive results that I'm finally getting, you don't have to waste the next thirty years searching; I already did that. You're welcome.

The Invisible Force

If you work hard enough for long enough, sometimes you get lucky. After years of study, trial, and error, I finally learned enough to put a system together that actually works. And it starts with understanding the following concept.

God created the universe, this world, and our brains to behave in a certain way. He set up universal laws, spiritual principles, and cause-and-effect relationships. Just like a computer or any other electronic device you may use every day, our brains and our universe function according to their design. And many of us have, albeit unknowingly, tried to operate the equipment, so to speak, in a manner that is not compatible with how that equipment was designed to function.

As anyone can imagine, no matter how hard you try or how many times you try or how loud you scream or what kind of language you discover is capable of escaping from your mouth, if you try to work a piece of equipment in a manner contrary to how it was designed to work, it will not do for you what you want it to do.

I doubt you'll really need to try this to be convinced. I'm sure you can imagine getting into your computer and trying to scan something—with your scanner turned off. You can try it a thousand times, but it won't work. (Don't ask me how I know this.) Or perhaps you could try pressing the Tab key instead of the Enter key, or clicking on bold instead of italics. You can try it a thousand times, and you will still not get the result you want—no matter how angry you become. You can even cry, scream, plead with and/or threaten your computer—and it will still not give you what you want, unless you can figure out how to work the equipment or program properly.

What you really need to do if you want optimal results from any program is to learn how that program was designed to operate. Then you can get the results you want with predictable and consistent accuracy. The same principle applies to operating your brain and your world. You can learn how to operate your brain properly and create your life experience with similar predictability and accuracy.

Some people come by this naturally. Each of us has our own unique set of talents and abilities. I just thought that because everything else seemed to come so easily to me that success in life should come easily to me as well. How wrong I was. This was a constant battle for most of my adult life, until I learned how things really work.

Like I said, if you keep trying to operate equipment—a computer program or anything else—in the wrong way, you get the wrong result. So, how do you operate your life in the right way to achieve success?

Well, if you're not one of the lucky ones who happened to be programmed for success early on—if you haven't been getting the results that you want out of life—if you feel like something outside of your control has been preventing you from becoming successful, then you first need to realize this:

> There is no supreme being that has decided to keep you down for the rest of your life, no matter what you do.

I know this may be a rhetorical statement for many people, but I also know what it's like to feel like no matter what I do, some spiritual force is not going to let me succeed. *Oh, yes. This supreme master will let other, less deserving people flourish, succeed, and be incredibly happy. But me? No, God has singled me out to torture for the rest of my life, and no matter what I do, I cannot possibly be good enough to make Him change His mind.*

Before you order me a straightjacket, I don't think I ever actually believed that to be the case. But I do know what it's like to feel that way. Just knowing intellectually that something can't be true doesn't always stop you from feeling that way.

Instead of believing that (or at least feeling like) you're doomed to a life of failure and misery because of some force beyond your control, you must trade that belief in for one more like this one:

> The universe operates according to natural, spiritual laws instituted by a loving God. Causes produce correlating effects. If I can learn how to put a given cause into action, that cause will produce the effect that correlates to that cause.

If you are not getting the effects you desire, you are not putting the correlating causes into action. That, or you are sabotaging your efforts with some conflicting cause. If you start putting the proper causes into action and eliminating conflicting ones, the correlating effects will necessarily occur—they have to by law! That sounds simple enough, but how do you change what causes you're putting into action?

The fact is, we don't see what goes on behind the scenes. There *is* actually an invisible force that controls our outcomes against our will—if we don't know how to "work the program." Yes, it is true that no matter how hard we try, how hard we work, how much we stress out, and even how much we pray—our results are often contrary to what we're trying to achieve. And the reason for this is that there is, indeed, an invisible force that works against us with much greater strength than we can work toward something.

The invisible force I'm referring to is your *subconscious mind*. Some of us were lucky and got good, productive programming in the area of being successful in life. But many of us, somehow or another, were programmed for failure in certain aspects of life. If you feel an invisible force holding you back, it's your subconscious programming sabotaging your success—not God singling you out for a life of torment and grief.

And the fact is, the subconscious mind is much more powerful than the conscious mind is. Experts have estimated that it's about 12 percent conscious to 88 percent subconscious. So, no matter how hard you try—well, imagine how hard it would be to win a tug-of-war with twelve people on your side and eighty-eight people on the opposing side. That's a pretty accurate comparison when it comes to what you're battling if your mind was programmed counterproductively.

And here's what's worse. You can't see the 88 percent—you think that the 12 percent that you're conscious of is all there is—because that's all you can see. But actually, the 88 percent works without your realizing it, hidden from your view, leaving behind effects that are often undesirable or even catastrophic, and leaving you wondering, *Why me?*

I thought for years that I was "Mr. Positive." I've even been referred to as "Mr. Positive" now and then (usually with sarcasm). I believed in thinking positively and thought that I was overall a very positive person. I had studied the subject fairly extensively and thought I understood it well.

For many years, I did not realize that even though I had made the conscious decision to believe and act in a positive way, subconsciously I had been programmed just the opposite way, when it comes to success in life. And the subconscious programming was consistently winning. Maybe not in every instance, but overall, the results were conclusive—my subconscious programming was much more effective than my conscious resolve.

Even when I thought I learned what I did wrong the last time, the next time it was something completely different. Most of the time, I was dealing with circumstances seemingly beyond my control. I could sense the invisible force sabotaging my success—but I couldn't see that the invisible force was my own subconscious mind!

When I found out about this "losing syndrome," believe it or not, I felt happy, relieved, and excited. I couldn't believe that this was something that happened with a fairly large number of people. It just felt like God was keeping me from being successful no matter how hard I tried, but He wouldn't tell me why. I had no idea that my subconscious programming was the invisible force that had been sabotaging my success all those years.

But when I found out what the problem was, I knew that there was a solution. You can reprogram the subconscious mind! You can learn how to operate the equipment—your brain—to give you the results you want. It isn't always as quick or as easy as you'd like. But, there are a number of things you can do to change the programming that has been sabotaging your life.

The good news is that this is something that is within your control. You *can* do it. It doesn't depend upon some imaginary, unfair, discriminating force that has singled you out as a permanent victim and delights in torturing your soul on a daily basis.

If you are reading this and can relate to some of the things I'm describing, you may have the same condition I had. And if so, be happy! Be absolutely thrilled! Because now you know what it is and that there is a cure! This should be fantastic news—the problem is correctable! You just have to learn how to correct it.

What is Success?

If you've now decided that your results in life to this point put you in the "loser" category, good! You know where you are. Now, let's figure out where you're going.

We all want to be successful, right? Well, if we want to become successful, we'd better decide what success is. How do you define success?

Earl Nightingale said, "Success is the progressive realization of a worthy ideal." That's an excellent definition—maybe the best one around. But I'd like to get a little more specific for our purposes here.

Yes, we want to acknowledge the importance of progress. Having a successful life means making consistent progress over many years. We're not going to just wake up one morning with everything completely different—then just stop right there for the rest of our lives. We're going to get to experience the joy and satisfaction of watching great things happen over time. And we need to notice and appreciate this progress.

But there is still something we're going to have in mind that we feel will make us *successful* at some given point in time and that is what we are trying to achieve.

I think we all have some set of circumstances in our minds that we know would make us feel like we have achieved success. Even if we want to continually progress, such that what would make us feel successful will change over time, there is still some position we want to be in that we believe will make us feel like we've achieved success. So let's talk about what that is.

And by the way, financial success is only one element of success in life. Real success is a lot bigger than how much money we have in the bank. So, what is success for our purpose here?

To me, success is not only the progress toward meeting a set of goals but is also the actual achievement of a certain level of satisfaction in life—a lifestyle or set of goals that I have already achieved, while I continue to progress toward other goals.

I guess I would define success in general terms as "a pattern of consistently achieving goals over time." But success to me in my life would include a list of things that are personal to me that would make me feel successful.

I want to keep things as simple as possible here, so I'm going to break down success, or the important things in life, into only three broad categories:

- Be
- Do
- Have

I think I can probably file everything that's important in life into one of these three categories. I know that it would be very easy to have many more categories, and you can do it that way if you like. I just wanted to keep it simple.

Be: Who and what do you want to be? Do you want to be a successful professional with a loving, devoted family and loyal friends? Do you want to be a person of high integrity with a certain set of moral values that you believe in and uphold? Maybe you want to be something that will allow you to live in a less stressful or less conventional way than those of us in the rat race.

I believe we should not just focus on how much money we want or where we want to live. We have a lot of our identity and self-worth tied up in what and who we are. This can include lots of things, most obviously our choice of careers. Do you want to be a doctor, lawyer, businessperson, teacher, artist, etc.? Or do you only want a certain income or lifestyle? I believe it's best to choose *what* you want to be, and then become successful at that thing.

As for *who* you want to be—do you want to be a kind, generous, honest person? Do you want to be lazy and undisciplined? You should set goals around what and who you want to be, so you don't become something or someone else accidentally.

Do: In addition to who and what you want to be, you can set goals detailing what you want to do in life. Perhaps you would like to travel the world and get to know other cultures and languages. Maybe there are talents you would like to develop. Maybe you want to be more active in church or community activities. I'll bet everyone reading this book has something they'd really like to do but haven't found a way to do yet.

If you're single, perhaps you want to get married and have a family. This can be big on the *do* list, but it can also be placed into the *be* or *have* categories.

Have: A certain level of financial security and success is important. After all, it's hard to be and do what you want without the financial resources to pay for the expenses involved. And many worthwhile goals do require a certain level of financial freedom. I'm confident that my future includes a significant amount of travel, and the time-freedom and lifestyle I have in mind are quite expensive.

There are lots of potential *haves*. This can include great health, wonderful relationships, financial security, a beautiful home, fancy cars, whatever is important to you.

Maybe you want to have more love in your life. I have yet to meet anyone who doesn't want love in some form or another. Everyone seems to want a significant other, family, and friends. Depending on where you are in life, this category still has relative importance when we're talking about the important things in life. It would be impossible for most of us to have a happy life without any relationships whatsoever. This is a very important *have*.

How about health? This is often taken for granted among the young and healthy, but it becomes a very high priority when it is threatened or taken away. In any case, it is hard to have a good life without good health. It is definitely something that should be a priority if you want to live a long and happy life.

We could go on and on about this. But if you decide on what you believe to be success in these three categories, set some goals, and start achieving these things, you should feel successful.

I should mention for the sake of completeness that it is important to have some balance in your life. So, if you're going to use the simple categories of *be, do,* and *have,* it's a good idea to consider the following areas when setting your goals so that you don't ignore an important aspect of life and let yourself get too out of balance:

1. Health/Fitness

2. Marriage/Family/Relationships

3. Financial Status

4. Spirituality

5. Education (Knowledge/Wisdom)

6. Career/Business Success

7. Personal Goals

When listing your goals, certain things can qualify in any category. That's okay. You can *have* great health or *be* very healthy, whichever you choose. And sometimes, in order to have something or to be something, you have to do something. However you choose to categorize these things is fine.

Success is certainly a journey—but in order to feel like you are successful, you generally have to have already accomplished something that you decide makes you a successful person. Success is most importantly how you view yourself, who you are, what you've done with your life so far—your identity.

As long as you have established a pattern of consistently achieving your goals and you are continuing in the right direction, I would say that you should consider yourself a success. Just keep up the good work in order to remain successful.

So we've talked about success and what it is. This is what we want—success in all the important aspects of our lives. We want money, but we don't want to sacrifice things that are even more important to get it. We want it all. So why don't we have it all?

You Were
Programmed to Fail

For the purposes of this book, I am assuming that you are one of the people I wrote this book for—someone with all the ability and drive necessary but without the results so far. That doesn't mean you've never succeeded at anything—it only means that you haven't yet been able to establish a long-term pattern of success in all the areas that are important to you.

Since we've now identified the invisible force preventing your success as your subconscious mind, let's talk about subconscious programming and how to fix it. This is extremely important to understand because this explains why you're not getting what you want out of life and how to change things so that you will from now on.

There is a filter between your conscious mind and your subconscious mind. This filter is quite effective at keeping things that enter your conscious mind from entering your subconscious mind, if those things are not compatible with what is already in the subconscious mind.

So how is there anything in your subconscious mind to begin with? Well, that filter became active over time. When you were born, your mind was a clean slate. Everything that entered the conscious mind just kept right on going, straight into the subconscious. I'm sure you have noticed how extremely impressionable young children are.

After some time, your subconscious has accepted a certain amount of programming. As this occurs, the filter kicks in and starts to reject suggestions that are not compatible with the information that was previously accepted.

Unfortunately, during the period of time in which you were most vulnerable to things entering your subconscious, you weren't aware that some pieces of information would be good for you and some would be bad for you. In addition, the people largely responsible for what entered your subconscious probably didn't understand this either.

Our parents, or whoever raised us from birth, had a huge influence on our subconscious programming. There were other influences too, of course. For most of us, our parents were just normal people who had problems and challenges and just did the best they could. But a little here and a little there, certain things entered our subconscious minds that may not be good for us, and they won't leave until we learn that there is a problem and how to fix it.

If something is programmed into the subconscious effectively, our brains accept it as truth. This perceived truth is taken as a strict order and our minds set out to obey this order, or to maintain the perceived required status.

For example, let's say that because of one messy drawing, a set of parents determines that their four-year-old son has absolutely no artistic talent. Without thinking, one of them makes a comment to the boy like, "Good thing you're so cute because your brother got all the talent."

The child's subconscious mind could accept that suggestion as absolute truth if there wasn't any contrary programming relating to that topic that was previously accepted. The boy's subconscious mind might then limit how well he performed in that category. It may be that he was actually blessed with incredible talent. Maybe it will even be accidentally discovered one day. But it is entirely possible that this negative programming will stay with this person for the rest of his life, limiting how well he is able to perform in that area.

Or perhaps his art will be good, but his perception of both its value and his probability of success will be such that he won't pursue his art like he should.

This happened to me with music. I always knew I had the talent, because I heard it from so many experts while I was growing up. But I think I didn't really believe that I could or should succeed at it because of the negative comments my mother made to me about being a professional musician while I was growing up.

At some point in life, experts say around seven to ten years old, your subconscious mind has enough information programmed into it that it starts becoming much more effective at keeping out any information that is incompatible with what's already been accepted as truth. In other words, the filter has kicked in.

The information accepted by the subconscious may be highly inaccurate and unnecessarily limiting, but the subconscious still accepts these pieces of information as commands that it is required to perform. So, just because you read about how you can become successful if you do A, B, C, and you decide to do it—that doesn't mean you'll be successful. Your success depends on whether your subconscious mind has been programmed to allow you to be successful, or if it is following its perceived orders to prevent you from becoming successful.

Remember that the efforts you make using your conscious mind may be fighting some conflicting piece of information that was programmed into your subconscious mind. And if this is the case, you're fighting 88 percent of your brain with only 12 percent of your brain. That's a ratio of approximately nine to one. You can guess which part will generally win that contest.

Identifying self-defeating behaviors can uncover some bad programming. If you have a bad habit, lack of self-confidence, a phobia, lack of focus on what you want, a bad temper—any aspect about yourself that you'd like to change—chances are, you were programmed with some piece of information that is counterproductive to your goals and desires.

And it wasn't all done by your parents; there are a number of other ways that something can slip through the filter and get stuck in your subconscious. But however the counterproductive programming got into your subconscious, once you become an adult, you are responsible for your own actions and your own life. That means it's up to you to identify what needs to change, and it's up to you to find a way to change it.

We must all accept this responsibility. Yes, we may have been programmed the wrong way when we were too young to be at fault. But if we dwell on how it happened instead of on what to do about it, we deny our ability to change our lives and to take charge of our own destiny.

It is very important to realize that you cannot see what has been programmed into your subconscious. The way you can tell what has been programmed into your subconscious is to examine your life. Are you where you want to be? Have you achieved what you set out to achieve? Are you satisfied with your direction and the results you've gotten so far? Are your relationships all that you imagined they would be? Are you happy, healthy, and prosperous? Are you the type of person that you believe you should be?

Your mind was programmed with lots of different pieces of information. And you may not want to change all of it. In my case, for example, my mother instilled in me some positive traits I'd like to keep. She taught me to be a caring, honest, and hardworking person. I don't need to reprogram that information. But there were other things that I would like to reprogram.

I think that most of us got a mixed bag when it comes to our subconscious programming. Some things we should probably keep and others we should probably reprogram. There may be some very good programming in your subconscious that makes you the kind of person you want to be. But there may also be some programming that has not served you well. If you have been programmed for failure instead of success, that part of your programming needs to be replaced.

Depending upon your background, there may be a lot of well-intentioned pieces of erroneous information that were crammed into your subconscious and that are now sabotaging any efforts you make to be successful.

Destructive core beliefs can cause your gut instincts to be wrong. They'll cause your judgment to be off. They will cause you to make the wrong decisions—even when you really, really try to make the right ones. And it's hard to be successful when your subconscious mind is carrying out orders to sabotage your success!

Here are some typical examples of destructive core beliefs, or bad subconscious programming, on the subject of success and prosperity:

1. It may not be God's will for me to be successful. If it's not God's will, I shouldn't pursue it and it won't work even if I do.

2. It is a sin to be rich. Most rich people will not go to heaven.

3. Rich people are greedy and dishonest. They take advantage of others and harm society.

4. A person cannot become rich without compromising their integrity. You can't be honest and get rich.

5. I am not capable of becoming a success.

6. I am not worthy of success.

7. It is noble to be poor.

8. Rich people think they're better than everyone else.

9. You have to have money to make money.

10. It is not possible to be both rich and happy. Rich people secretly lead lonely, miserable lives.

11. Success is not in our family—you have to be born into the right family to be wealthy and successful.

12. It's a zero-sum game—if you have more than you need, you're causing someone else to have less than they need.

13. Being wealthy is wrong because those who have extra should give it all away to the poor.

14. Desiring wealth and success is wrong—you should only desire to be a good person with enough to get by.

15. It is wrong for some people to have more than others.

16. You have to be lucky to get rich—and I'm just not that lucky.

17. To become wealthy, you have to sacrifice family life and work non-stop. It's better to spend that time with family and just not worry about being a success.

18. Becoming wealthy would just cause more problems. A "simple life" is much better.

19. Coming into money changes a person into something bad.

20. Money is the root of all evil.

21. I don't have the education or breeding to become rich.

22. I would be very uncomfortable being rich—I'm laid back, not stuffy and pretentious.

23. It's dangerous to be rich—you always have to look over your shoulder.

24. I'll have a bigger reward in heaven if I suffer faithfully on earth.

25. If God wanted me to be rich, I would have won the lottery already.

26. You can't control fate—what will happen will happen and there's nothing you can do to change it.

27. It's too late for me. If something big were going to happen in my life, it would have happened by now.

The list goes on forever, but you get the idea. Obviously, all of the above statements are false—but if your subconscious believes them, this will affect your ability to be successful.

We need to replace negative subconscious beliefs with positive ones. When it comes to success and prosperity, we need to get rid of the type of beliefs listed above and replace them with some like these:

1. God and the universe want me to succeed.

2. To succeed and prosper is a noble and worthy pursuit.

3. I can be of more value to society if I am successful and prosperous.

4. It is my destiny to be happy, healthy and successful.

5. I am worthy of success and happiness.

6. I can be rich—and happy—and a good person.

7. I am comfortable with wealth and success.

8. I allow myself to be highly successful.

9. I am a winner—I rise above all challenges.

10. Life is an exciting adventure and I live mine to the fullest.

Programming these beliefs and similar ones into your subconscious will help to get rid of the false, limiting beliefs—and this will stop your subconscious mind from sabotaging your success. When your mind is working toward your success instead of fighting against it, your gut instincts and intuition about what actions to take will contribute to your success instead of preventing it.

Very shortly, we will go over exactly what you need to do in order to replace negative core beliefs with positive ones. After you've installed better core beliefs about success, you can use the steps I will outline to achieve specific goals, and you will be much more effective at achieving your goals than you have been in the past. Like I said before, when you understand how to work the equipment (your mind), it is a lot easier to get the results you're looking for.

The Definition of *Want*

We've talked a little bit about the problem of consistently *not* achieving what we want to in life. And we can define the cause of this problem as counter-productive subconscious programming.

Before we get into the solution, I want to redefine the word *want*. We think we know what this word means. What we consciously desire, we *want*. That is correct, of course. But that is only the definition to our conscious minds. As far as our subconscious minds are concerned, there is a completely different definition.

Your subconscious mind wants to protect you and to serve you. And when you have a certain piece of information about yourself programmed into your subconscious, your mind accepts that information as an order that it must obey or a status that it must protect. This becomes what your subconscious mind *wants*—even if it is the exact opposite of what your conscious mind wants.

For example, if you are a student and your subconscious mind is programmed to get all Bs in school, your subconscious mind *wants* to get all Bs. It will cause you to study more and retain information better if you're at risk to get a C, and it will cause you to be distracted or work less if you're at risk of getting an A.

It *wants* to make sure you get a B because it wants to serve you, and it believes that it is serving you best by making sure you get a B. It believes that this is the best scenario for you, because that's what it was programmed to believe.

Has anyone ever told you when something undesirable happened to you, "Subconsciously, you wanted that to happen"? That does sound pretty offensive, doesn't it? But there may be a lot of truth in that statement. You have to realize that the word *want* means two different things to your conscious and subconscious minds.

Imagine you're in a fight against a group of nine ninja warriors, all well trained and focused on their objective: to disable you. You against nine. Who do you think will win?

To make matters worse, now imagine that the nine ninjas are invisible. Do you really think you'll have a chance against them? Not likely, right? (Remember that 88 percent to 12 percent is roughly the same as a 9:1 ratio of the power of your subconscious mind vs. your conscious mind—and the subconscious is hidden from your view.)

Well, now imagine that as these highly-skilled warriors are coming at you, they all stop suddenly and appear to be listening to their respective earpieces—then they all smile at you and say, "Oh, we're supposed to be protecting you, not beating the crap out of you. Excellent—we'll help you to safely get exactly where you want to go."

That's how the subconscious mind works. It *wants* what it is programmed to *want*. Even if that's not what you want consciously—it believes that it can serve and protect you best by doing what it was programmed to do for you. Since it wants to serve you, it *wants* whatever it is programmed to believe it is supposed to do for you. And it is very effective at getting what it *wants*.

This concept is very important to understand. If you were programmed for failure instead of for success, you will have a very hard time consistently achieving your goals, because your subconscious mind will sabotage your efforts. No matter how hard you try, you won't connect with your goals because your subconscious, with roughly a nine to one ratio, will prevent you from attaining them, all the while allowing you to think that you did your best but the situation was simply out of your control.

After establishing a pattern of not being able to attain your goals, you will believe that all of your circumstances are beyond your control and you simply cannot become successful, for reasons you can't understand or change.

What's actually happening is that even though you want something consciously, you *want* the opposite subconsciously, and because your subconscious thoughts are hidden from your conscious mind, you won't know exactly what your subconscious mind is doing to sabotage your success. You probably won't even know that your subconscious mind is doing anything to sabotage your success.

You will simply know that you are consistently unable to achieve your goals. And you might feel like things just don't go right for you. Then your mind will try to make sense of this information by speculating as to why this is. There's a dark cloud over you, failure runs in the family, you're being punished by God, anything that allows your conscious mind to believe it understands why you fail.

Because your subconscious mind will sabotage your conscious efforts to succeed until it is reprogrammed, it may be a complete waste of time to learn how to set goals and take action—until after you reprogram your mind with new core beliefs that will help you to get what you want out of life, instead of preventing you from getting what you want.

You must first reprogram your subconscious mind for success—then your mind will help you to succeed instead of preventing you from succeeding. (Remember the ninjas.) Then, when you set goals and start taking actions to achieve them, your subconscious mind will direct you to take actions that will help you succeed, instead of directing you to take actions that will guarantee your failure.

If you have consistently taken actions based on your gut feelings, "inspiration," what you truly believe to be the right choices, or any other method of making your choices—but your choices consistently do not result in success, this is why. You need to reprogram your mind to allow you to be successful—and to make you successful—then set your goals, take your actions, and success will come naturally.

Section 2:
The Solution

We've identified the problem.

So how do we fix this long-term losing streak? Well, first we have to reprogram the core beliefs of your subconscious mind. Not all of them—just the ones that are limiting your success. Of course, if there are other behaviors or attitudes that you believe should be improved, you can reprogram those as well.

Once you've at least started to turn around what your subconscious mind believes about you and whether it should allow you to be successful or not, we can focus on achieving specific goals. The process of reprogramming your core subconscious beliefs is very similar to the process of programming your subconscious mind to help you to achieve your goals. So for now, a lot of the info we're about to cover will apply to both.

Reprogramming
Your Subconscious

We already identified some counter-productive core beliefs about success that may have been programmed into your subconscious mind. Since you can't simply take a look inside and see what's in there, you have to go by your long-term results in order to determine what kind of programming actually took place in your past. If you're not successful in life, that's a pretty clear indication that you were not programmed to succeed.

We also specified a short list of positive core beliefs about success that you can install in your subconscious in such a way as to push out the negative beliefs that have been there a long time, and be left with only beliefs that will help you to become successful. These positive beliefs are contrary to the negative beliefs that you might have in your subconscious mind right now, so trading your old beliefs in for these new ones will have a big impact on your results.

Though what you think in your conscious mind is certainly important, real change comes through reprogramming the subconscious mind. So, how do you exchange your destructive, old subconscious beliefs for the positive new ones? There are a number of ways to reprogram the subconscious.

The most obvious way to change your subconscious programming is with hypnosis. I studied hypnosis extensively and have used this tool successfully to help people change their subconscious programming. I do not believe it to be evil, mysterious, or dangerous as long as it's used properly. In fact, it has proven to be very helpful for the people I hypnotize.

Simply put, hypnosis is an effective way to reprogram what was programmed wrong to begin with. If you're against hypnosis, you probably never studied it, and you may not have all the facts. In reality, it may be very different than you think.

There isn't a person alive whose subconscious hasn't been programmed. It happens without your knowledge or permission, when you're too young to understand what's going on. And if you were programmed counterproductively, you should probably want to repair that damage by reprogramming. Hypnosis is one effective way to reprogram your subconscious mind.

In addition to being programmed as children, without our knowledge, there are also things that can affect our programming as adults. Something stressful, traumatic, repetitive, or something that makes a very strong impression on us—these things can sneak past the gatekeeper and into the subconscious. Or something we're not paying attention to, while we are paying attention to something else—this can create a diversion for the conscious mind and allow the filter to be open while something passes through it.

Hypnosis is simply a method of making suggestions to the subconscious mind while in a state of suggestibility, so that the subconscious mind will allow those suggestions to be received instead of being rejected by the filter. The idea is to be able to choose your own programming instead of being a victim of programming you really don't want.

Whether you realize it or not, you have already put yourself in that state of suggestibility without even knowing it. Have you ever "zoned out"? Ever daydreamed? Ever been so captivated by a book, movie, piece of music, or thought, that you were just kind of somewhere else? Well, you were in a state of suggestibility or hypnosis. Hypnotists have a way of putting you into that state then speaking suggestions to your subconscious mind that are meant to benefit you in some way.

If you put enough of these positive suggestions into your subconscious, they will eventually override the previous negative programming that the new programming conflicts with, and the negative programming will be rejected and dismissed.

You can do this with the help of a professional hypnotherapist, or you can use self-hypnosis. Or, you don't have to use what you think of as hypnosis at all. Any way that you can find yourself in a suggestible state will allow your subconscious to accept suggestions of your choosing, as opposed to keeping those suggestions your brain accepted that were not by your choosing.

I am not going to teach you how to hypnotize your-self or anyone else—I just wanted to address the subject briefly because misconceptions about hypnosis are so prevalent. If you have all the abilities you need to be a winner but you find that after years of hard work you're still a loser—it's because of your subconscious program-ming. Reprogramming by one method or another is nec-essary if you want to change your results.

Whether you are comfortable with hypnosis or not, there are other ways to achieve the results you desire. Just realize that what you are trying to do is to reprogram your subconscious mind. If your subconscious programming is causing you to fail, you must change your programming if you want to succeed.

Another thing we mentioned that can help to repro-gram your subconscious mind is *repetition*. If you say, hear, think, write, or see something enough times, some of it will eventually get past the filter and sink into your sub-conscious mind.

This is the idea behind *affirmations*. You write a state-ment that you want to be true, phrase it in the present and positive, add positive emotions, and speak it to yourself over and over again over time.

For example, you could start saying to yourself 100 times per day, "I enjoy my job, and I'm the best at what I do." After a reasonable period of time, that should have some positive effect on your attitude toward your job and the quality of your work. The new thought will gradually replace your pre-vious programming if you're persistent and do it right.

Many systems, books, teachings, etc. suggest engaging in something like affirmations. Many also teach *visualiza-*

tion, holding on to a picture of some thing that you want or some situation as you want it to be. This can also have a positive effect. But it might be hard to find a system that combines all the right elements in the most effective way. I hope to accomplish that in this book.

If you want to get from point A to point B, you have to point yourself in the right direction and move forward. If you're in a car, you have to manipulate the steering wheel so that you're headed in the direction you want to go, and you also must step on the gas so that the car will actually move in that direction.

The same applies here. If you feel that you have the ability to be a winner (one who wins most of the time) but your present circumstances suggest that you have been programmed to be a loser (one who loses most of the time), you must point yourself in the right direction then actually move in that direction at a reasonable speed. How do you do that?

Direction:

There are four things that you need to combine in order to make a dramatic enough impression in your brain to get past the gatekeeper (filter) standing in front of your subconscious mind:

1. Thoughts
2. Words
3. Pictures
4. Emotions

I believe that one of the reasons some of the other programs I tried didn't really work for me is that one or more of these elements was missing or wasn't explained thoroughly.

Thoughts

The things that enter your mind and that you dwell upon are extremely important. The first thing you should do is to limit what even has the opportunity to enter your mind.

What kind of information are you allowing to enter your mind? Does it have value? Is it high-quality information? Does it lead you to believe and to feel that you are a highly capable person with unlimited opportunity, or does that information suggest that you are incapable, that you've missed the boat, or that opportunities simply don't exist for you right now?

Learn to change the subject, shut off the news, stop watching that DVD, etc., and pick up a positive book, listen to something encouraging, study successful people, etc. If you're trying to lose weight, you have to refuse to allow that delicious donut to enter your mouth. In the same way, if you're trying to change the way you think, you have to refuse to allow certain types of input to enter your brain.

In addition to what enters your mind from external sources, you have to monitor what you dwell upon. Have you ever gone through some unlikely scenario in your mind that was really negative? Some way you'd react if someone pushed your buttons or confronted you in an aggressive way or anything like that? If you have, you know that after a few minutes, you can get really emotional about a situation that will probably never happen and probably only would if you continue to dwell upon it.

You need to have something positive prepared and ready in advance to replace any negative thought that may creep in.

For example, if you find yourself in the shower one morning thinking to yourself, *"I really don't want to go to work today; this is going to be a lousy day; if my boss brings up that issue with me one more time I'm going to…",* have something ready to replace it. Catch yourself and say, "Self—I notice that I'm dwelling on the negative and that's not the direction I want to go. So, I'm going to change the subject. This is going to be a fantastic day! Things are going to go right, and if something does go wrong, I'm going to find a solution to the problem. At the end of the day, I'm going to feel very satisfied."

Control what information you allow to enter your mind and what you dwell upon. You can catch yourself thinking counterproductively and decide to change what you're thinking about or how you're thinking about it. You simply have something else ready to think about and swap out those thoughts.

Words

The words you speak are very important. The Bible makes numerous references to the power of the tongue. Just like you have to watch what you think about, you also have to watch what you say. If you go around all day saying, "I'm just so tired all the time—I don't understand it," you're going to be more tired than if you walk around saying, "I can't believe how much energy I have today!"

With our words, we prophesy our future. We must be careful how we speak. This will take practice to implement and study to understand the extent of the importance and effectiveness of this concept.

Pictures/Visualization

You move in the direction of what you dwell upon. Using mental pictures is one of the most effective ways to dwell upon something and point yourself in that direction. If you consistently visualize a specific improvement in your life, whether it's a new car, home, job, or whatever, you are more likely to realize the improvement you seek.

On the other hand, visualization, in addition to your thoughts, words, and emotions, is easy to use in a counterproductive way. If you're not disciplined enough to catch yourself when you're visualizing something you don't want, you'll continue to visualize what you don't want instead of making yourself visualize what you do want. You point yourself in the direction of what you visualize.

Emotions

This one is very important but often overlooked. We are all largely governed by our emotions. And few people have developed a strong ability to control their own emotions. Most people allow their emotions to come and go as they will, and they point themselves in a direction they don't want to go, because their emotions are undisciplined.

Emotions create a magnetic force between you and what you associate to the emotion. One of the most powerful things you can do to attract what you want—or what you don't want—into your life is to use your mind to create the emotions you would feel if you were already in that situation. Remember Job? "What I was afraid of has come on me. What I worried about has happened to me." (Job 3:25 NIRV) Fortunately, this works for positive things too.

What we need to do is combine all four of these elements around some goal or desired belief. For example, let's say it's a financial goal. Let's say that you decide you want to save two thousand dollars to take your wife away for a long weekend on a surprise romantic getaway. You would combine all four elements something like this:

First, you need to dwell on already having the two thousand dollars. You don't want to keep pushing the two thousand dollars out into your future. If you do, your subconscious mind will keep it in your future. You want to put the two thousand dollars in your present—you want to think about having it in your hands right now.

Second, you want to speak the words out loud. "I have two thousand dollars right now for a romantic getaway." Do this as often as possible, combining all four elements at the same time.

Third, you want to visualize the two thousand dollars being in your hands right now. Visualize carrying your sweetheart over the threshold into your beautiful suite with the fantastic view. Imagine getting dressed up in the hotel room for the fancy dinner you're about to take her to. Picture it happening exactly the way you want it to happen.

Fourth—and here's where it all comes together—feel the emotions you would have if this were happening to you right now. Close your eyes and imagine opening up your hands to discover two thousand dollars in cash. Imagine exactly how you would feel if this were going on right now. Imagine how you would feel if you were to walk through the door right now and say, "Honey, pack your bags—I'm taking you away for our anniversary." Stop for a moment and imagine yourself in that situation and *feel* the emotions you would feel if you could do that right now.

Go through the whole experience, putting the bags in the car, driving to wherever you're going, checking into the hotel—whatever it is you want—don't just picture it; take the time to feel the emotions that would go along with your being in that situation right now.

If you simply imagine a picture of what something would look like at some undetermined time in the future, it doesn't cause as much emotion. If you can imagine and visualize dropping what you're doing right this second and engaging in whatever it is you want to do and take the time to experience the emotions you would feel if it were happening right now, this emotional component will supercharge your effectiveness.

Warning

By the way, be careful about one thing. There's a common mistake that can prevent you from obtaining the goals you visualize. It is actually easiest when you are visualizing your goals, to create emotions of want—the feeling of desire for, and lack of, the thing you're visualizing. It's natural to think that this is the correct way to go about this process, but it is actually one of the reasons that people fail.

You must understand that the conscious feeling of desire or want often translates into the subconscious as the belief of lack. When you visualize your goal, you must visualize already having it—not wanting to have it or wishing you could have it. If you visualize wanting whatever your goal happens to be, that feeling of want is reinforcing in your subconscious mind that you do *not* have what you desire. When creating emotions to attach to your pictures of what you want, remember that you must create the positive feelings associated with already having it—not the desire to obtain it.

Obviously, if you don't consciously desire something, you won't have any reason to pursue it or to try to attract it. But when you catch yourself feeling the lack of it while thinking about your desire, remember to imagine already having it—not wanting it.

Remember that your subconscious mind is a goal-seeking machine that follows orders without asking questions. If you program into your mind that you lack something, your subconscious will go to great lengths to make sure that you remain in a state of not having the item or goal you desire. You have to get used to creating and experiencing the positive emotions associated with having already obtained and currently enjoying what you desire.

If you want a tropical vacation, imagine yourself there on the beach, having servers bring you a pina colada—not looking through magazines wishing you could go. If you want a red Ferrari, imagine yourself driving one out of your garage—not looking at one through the dealership window.

This is a very important concept—don't program yourself to *not* have what you want. And don't keep it in the future—imagine having it *now*! Right now—not tomorrow and not next week!

Moving Forward:

After you set your direction, you still have to move forward. This will apply more to goal setting than to core belief reprogramming, because reaching specific goals involves taking specific actions that may not be necessary when simply trying to change attitudes, but the overall process is very similar.

The fact is, doing the four things above will cause you to move in the direction that you set. But you need to move with some kind of speed if you want to actually get somewhere. In a car, you put it in gear and step on the gas; you don't just let it idle along at two miles per hour. How do you do that with your goals? Here are two components of moving ahead at a reasonable speed:

1. Wisdom (Knowing what actions to take and/or not to take)

2. Actions (Taking the appropriate actions)

Let's talk about wisdom first. I'm sure I learned this from some source I can't even remember, but my definition of wisdom is *applied knowledge* or *applied education*. You have to have the knowledge, of course, but then you also have to have the good judgment to be able to apply it to a situation properly.

For our purposes, I would describe wisdom as the ability to set the right goal and then break the objective down into realistic steps that will result in the fulfillment of that goal. Wisdom is knowing what actions to take—or not to take.

As part of this wisdom, you may want to recognize that when you're dealing with the subconscious mind, you don't necessarily have to know everything you'll need to do in advance. If you program yourself to achieve an end result, you may not ever consciously know every single thing that went into its fulfillment.

It can be argued that simply programming your mind to achieve a certain thing is sufficient, and you are best off by simply allowing your subconscious to do its job and not worrying about how the thing will be accomplished.

However, gaining wisdom also means becoming educated about how to do what it is you have set out to do. Actions must be taken, whether by accident due to subconscious programming or by deliberate planning, and most effectively by a combination of the two, with your subconscious and conscious minds working synergistically instead of fighting each other.

I believe that you will be most effective when taking a determined action, but realizing at the same time that sometimes it is not those actions that are most effective in accomplishing your goals – and that if your mind is programmed effectively, it can sometimes lead you in a different direction, which may make you more effective in accomplishing your goal.

When your subconscious mind is programmed productively, you can trust it to lead you in the right direction. You can tell by your results whether you should trust in your intuition or whether you should "do the opposite" (more on this later) until you have successfully reprogrammed your subconscious mind.

Taking action doesn't really need to be defined. But it is important to use wisdom in what actions are taken. I spent years of my life spinning my wheels and wearing myself out because I took lots of actions, but those actions did not result in the fulfillment of my overall long-term objectives.

In the same way that we combine thoughts, words, mental pictures, and emotions in setting our direction, we also combine wisdom and actions in setting our velocity. If we point ourselves in the right direction and barely move, we've accomplished little to nothing. But if we can get good at setting our direction and good at learning how to move ahead at a faster pace, now we're getting somewhere.

Activity will not ensure success—I proved that. The right activities at the right time in the right way—with the right degree of persistence—more wisdom here—that's what will ensure success.

Faith and the Subconscious

Jesus was brilliant. But He didn't force-feed His messages to the people. In fact, He often spoke in such a way that some would understand and others would be confused. And sometimes, you might have to read or hear something He said many times before you actually "get it."

One of my favorite scripture verses is Mark 11:24. In this verse, Jesus said, "So I tell you, when you pray for something, believe that you have already received it. Then it will be yours (NIRV)."

The meaning of this verse often escapes people (especially when using translations that are not as clear as the NIRV is when it comes to this specific verse). Jesus is clearly stating that if you believe that you have already received what you're asking for (received in the recent past/now have in the present), you will receive it (future).

This short and simple verse actually contains a whole bunch of information if you think about it. For one thing, it might completely change the way you pray.

Many people pray from a feeling of lack. They ask God for something that they believe they do not have. And many times, the way they pray actually reinforces the emotions of lacking what they are praying for. If it's important or urgent, many times a person will cry out to God with great emotion, believing that their prayers will have the maximum possible effectiveness because of the energy and emotion they put into them.

But if you listen to what they're saying and sense what they're feeling when they're saying it, it is clear that they're asking, while *not* believing that they have already received what they're praying for. They're actually creating and experiencing the emotions of *not* having what they want.

Jesus said that we are to ask, believing that we have already received. Instead of pleading with God to grant you something that you strongly feel the lack of—frustrated that you still don't have it yet, somehow you need to be able to believe that you have already received the thing you are asking for. Then your approach will be entirely different.

To illustrate the vast difference between these two approaches, let's imagine two different scenarios for a moment. For our example, let's say that you have an exam coming up and that it is a very important exam. This exam could make or break your academic or working career. To you, it's the most important thing imaginable.

To complicate things further, let's say that your pre-tests didn't go very well. Let's say you're having trouble with certain subjects that will be on this test. You just haven't been able to fully grasp, use, or memorize the material you need to.

Many praying people would respond by sincere, emotional prayer; maybe even some tears, definitely some gut-wrenching pleadings that God would intervene—because you know if He doesn't, there's no way on earth you can possibly pass this exam. You create a presentation before God that you feel is the best you can possibly do because you invested so much of yourself into it.

But you got it all wrong. You came at it from the viewpoint of failure, not success. I'm going to interject an important concept here:

You don't always get what you want, need, deserve, or ask for—you get what you believe or expect—what your subconscious has been programmed to "want"! This is what you actually have faith in—and this is how faith works.

Jesus stated it plainly—you can have what you ask for, but you have to pray, believing that you have *already* received it!

Instead of emphasizing how horrible it feels to not have the thing you need or desire, a better approach would be to pray with a calm smile on your face—with no stress, no gut-wrenching pleadings, being perfectly relaxed, from a perspective of gratitude, not lack.

Put yourself in the example for a minute and think about this. If you truly believe that you have already passed the test—it's done; you passed; all is well; you got the internship, license, promotion—whatever. If you believe 100 percent that you've already passed the exam, do you cry out to God like you're about to be pounced on by a mountain lion, or do you joyfully and enthusiastically thank Him for helping you through this difficult exam, because it went extremely well and you accomplished what you set out to do?

I know that many of you reading this book don't necessarily believe in God. But for those of you who do, this may interest you. I have almost entirely stopped asking God for things. I never had a whole lot of luck when I did—it usually just frustrated me. Approaching God from the aspect of lack was never very effective for me.

I found that I got much better results when I started thanking Him in advance. The fact is, if I truly believe that I already have what I'm asking for, I feel more inclined to thank Him for it than I do to ask Him for it. After all, I already have it, don't I?

This is not to say that I never ask for anything—but when I do, I assume a positive response and thank Him for it before I close. Given the choice, I believe that assuming a positive response is much more productive than assuming a negative one.

For me, this thanking approach is so much more positive than an asking one, that my entire mood changes. It helps me to feel abundance, not lack. And a feeling of abundance creates more abundance; a feeling of lack creates more lack.

When I was teaching my wonderful wife this important concept, I wrote the following on a small memo pad and pinned it up on the kitchen wall, where it remains to this day:

> Today, I will think only positive thoughts;
> because if I think of only positive things today,

I will be happy today, and my happiness will attract more positive things into my life.

The fact is: a positive approach, coming from the perspective of abundance instead of lack, is much more effective in getting you what you want than a negative approach is. Try them both—you'll see the difference.

Reprogram Core Beliefs First

Before we go further into how to achieve specific goals, I want to talk more about how to reprogram your core subconscious beliefs. Doing at least some of this first will make goal achievement much easier and more realistic and far less frustrating.

This may not be the first book you have ever picked up on the subject of becoming successful. You may have been through a lot of different systems and still not found something that really works for *you*.

If so, why do you suppose that is? It is probably not because those books or seminars were bad. But they were probably incomplete, because they probably didn't teach you that you need to do the prerequisite reprogramming of some of your core subconscious beliefs before you set out to achieve goals that your subconscious mind was pre-programmed to prevent you from achieving.

The first thing to do is to get your subconscious mind working with you instead of against you. Then achieving goals becomes much easier. Once you've reprogrammed what your subconscious believes about you and your ability to become successful, achieving goals becomes natural instead of being an exhausting, almost impossible task.

The main difference between reprogramming core subconscious beliefs and programming the subconscious to achieve specific goals is that achieving specific goals usually includes taking some specific actions; whereas reprogramming your core subconscious beliefs is usually just about changing the way you think. Of course, your actions will change naturally as you change the way you think, but it is not usually necessary to include action steps in this process.

When it comes to changing the way we think, even if it's not an unfamiliar concept, most people have not been shown how to do this effectively. Many times, a person will read a book or attend a seminar then decide to change their thinking. So they start adding a little something extra to their thinking on a daily basis. They'll read something every day—once. Or they'll repeat an affirmation or two—once or twice. Something like that. Everything else about the way they think on a daily basis stays the same. Then, eventually they'll get distracted by something, stop doing it, and just decide it didn't work.

I want to use an analogy to explain what I'm suggesting here. Let's say I pick up a glass, put in some water, some dirt, and some sand. Then I stir it up and set the glass down in the sink. The glass represents your subconscious mind, and the dirt and sand represent your negative programming.

If I turn the faucet on a low setting and let clean water start to go into the already full glass, the dirty water will start leaving the glass by going over the sides. In other words, by forcing clean water in, I'm forcing dirty water out.

Your mind is like this: by putting positive thoughts into it consistently, negative thinking patterns will gradually leave. But here's the part I really want to emphasize. You will notice that the sand remains at the bottom of the glass. Why? Because of the low flow of the water going into the glass.

The sand represents your core subconscious beliefs. A very low flow of water volume going into the glass is just not enough to get rid of those deeply programmed, stubborn beliefs about yourself. If you do nothing but add a low flow of something positive to your thinking every day, it may make some difference—but probably not enough to dramatically change your world.

What you need to do is turn up the faucet to full-blast. Now watch the sand flow over the edges of the glass. This is what you need to do with your thoughts. You need to completely change what you allow to enter your mind and what you dwell upon.

Yes, this is different than what your family and friends do. It will take some getting used to. But at least for some amount of time in the beginning, if you really want to make a dramatic change in your programming, you need to flood your mind with positive thoughts and refuse to let anything negative remain there.

That may mean turning off the TV and listening to or reading something positive and motivational. Start referring to the news as "the bad news" as a reminder to be careful about what you let enter your brain. You don't really need to hear about every single negative thing that happens anywhere in the world every day, do you? Can you improve life for anybody by paying attention to every bad thing that happens to everyone everywhere?

Maybe you'll have to stop listening to the same people every day who only know how to complain. You will definitely want to prepare some positive phrases and mental pictures to have ready for whenever you find yourself thinking something negative and you need something fast to replace those negative thoughts with.

What you'll want to do when you're in the process of changing your core subconscious beliefs is to flood your mind with the things you want in there and starve your mind of the junk you want out of there. Yes, it is different and will be uncomfortable at first. But remember this:

> If you want your life to be dramatically superior to the average and ordinary lives you see around you, you have to do things dramatically differently than how average and ordinary people do them.

This statement is not intended to be judgmental or elitist; I'm only talking about how to get the results you want out of life. Don't feel guilty about wanting to have a fantastic life—that's what you should want and what you should have! Decide to be comfortable with that.

How to Reprogram Your Core Beliefs

There are a number of things you can do to reprogram your core subconscious beliefs. There are, of course, techniques that require the services a professional subconscious reprogrammer like myself; but this book is about what you can do on your own. Here's what I suggest:

First, by observing your life, you decide what beliefs are there that you want to get rid of.

Second, write an opposing belief that you want to install which will force out the current belief.

Third, flood your mind with the new belief in a variety of powerful ways so that the existing belief is forced out of your mind and your subconscious now accepts the new belief as truth. Utilize thoughts, words, pictures and emotions, as we discussed earlier.

Now, your subconscious mind will accept each belief you decided to program into it as an order that it must obey. It will manipulate you into acting in such a way as to become a winner instead of a loser—if that's what you program into it.

Earlier, I wrote out some negative beliefs you may have been programmed with and some positive ones to replace them with. Unless you believe that you can come up with some that better fit your situation, I suggest using the positive statements I provided. Flood your mind with these positive beliefs, in order to force the negative ones out and be left with programming that will help you to succeed instead of programming that will sabotage your success.

So, what are the most effective ways to flood your mind with these positive beliefs? Here are some ways that you can flood your mind with your chosen suggestions or otherwise effectively replace negative beliefs with positive ones:

1. Repetition. I suggest keeping your chosen positive beliefs on a 3x5 card in your pocket or purse. Anytime you have a spare moment—waiting in line, at a red light, walking, waiting on hold on the phone, during commercials if you're watching TV, etc.—read your list of beliefs. When it is feasible to do so, read them out loud—speak what you want to happen.

2. Bedtime. The last few minutes before you drift off to sleep, your subconscious mind is especially suggestible. I recommend reading, writing, and speaking your new beliefs just before sleeping and dwelling on them as you drift off to sleep.

3. Writing. We talked about how speaking, visualizing, etc. can help to get a chosen thought into the subconscious.

But did you know that writing something out can also have an effect? Handwriting experts can tell many things about a person by having them write something out on a piece of paper. And handwriting can change with different emotional states.

Did you know that this also works in reverse? If you learn to write something a little differently, it can actually affect the correlating trait in your mind.

If writing can have an effect on the subconscious, why not write out your new beliefs every night just before bed? You can keep a notebook by your bed and use a different page or half-page every night. After you fill up the notebook, you'll see how much you did to influence your mind to adopt the beliefs you chose—and replace those undesired beliefs that you were programmed with that you didn't choose. If you're only working with one or two new beliefs at a time, you can write them out ten or twenty times each—remember that repetition helps too.

4. Relaxing. Your mind becomes more receptive to suggestion when it's in a relaxed state—when your brainwaves are at a speed referred to as the *alpha state* (approx. 8-12 Hz). If you can find a time and place every day to sit or lie down, without falling asleep, and relax while visualizing yourself as if you presently had the programming you desire—and the effects you want your new programming to produce, this will have a positive effect on your new programming.

5. NLP. If you study Neuro-Linguistic Programming, you'll learn some techniques that can cause certain types of changes to occur very quickly. Or a NLP practitioner can do some exercises or procedures with you and you won't have to study it and become an expert yourself. NLP techniques are very often a shortcut that can result in a faster change than many other methods of making certain types of internal changes.

   Unless you have an interest in helping others by becoming a certified NLP Practitioner and are willing to devote the required investment of time and money, I suggest hiring a professional NLP Practitioner to assist you with meeting your own personal goals.

6. Sing (or rap, if you must). Music is a great way to get words into your head. That's why advertisers have been using it for years. Sometimes it's hard to get a song out of your head—even if you hate it! Phrase your new beliefs so that you can repeat them over and over again very easily by making up tunes in your head or by singing them to music you listen to in your car, etc.

   You can also do the same thing without actually using a melody—keeping the words in an easily repeatable rhythm makes it very easy to keep the repetition going. You can do this using the beat of music you happen to be listening to, or any beat or rhythm you can remember or create in your head. Yes, any of these options will sound ridiculous to others, so you may want to keep this to yourself.

The Bible talks a lot about the power of the tongue (See Proverbs 18:21; 12:25; 21:23; Psalm 141:3). Perhaps I take this too literally, but I don't think so. I believe that a person can walk around repeating affirmations simply by moving the tongue inside their closed mouth, without making a sound or even moving their lips noticeably, and still be effective.

This is great when in you're public, anytime you feel you're wasting time with some meaningless activity or are stuck with unwanted time to kill. You're still causing your mind to repeat an idea by creating words with your tongue. Even though it is not noticeable to anyone else, it is still an effective way to use the repetition of affirmations to get an idea into your subconscious mind.

One thing you can do to increase your use of this technique is to put a clock on your nightstand that actually makes a ticking sound every second. This creates a sixty-beat-per-minute metronome that will make it very easy to repeat an affirmation to yourself when you're falling asleep or waking up—both good times to get an idea into the subconscious.

7. Emotional Release Techniques. I learned a simple technique a while back called The Sedona Method, which I found to be helpful in releasing negative, or counterproductive, emotions. Not surprisingly, when you learn

how to allow these negative emotions to leave you, it's easier to experience positive emotions, which will help you to achieve positive results in your life.

This technique is easy to learn and simple to use. It does not require paying a professional for consultations, only paying for the course up front. I found it to be well worth the cost of the program, as it helped me to reduce my stress level at a time when I really needed to.

Meridian Tapping is another emotional release technique that is reported to have some very positive results. This may be a little more involved to learn than The Sedona Method, as there are expensive classes available to help you master the technique and practitioners available as well, but it is a very simple concept.

8. Time Line Therapy®. This is a highly effective modality that is designed to make rapid changes in the way your mind perceives past events and to change the effects those events have on your present and future experience. In addition, you can actually place desired events into your future, and your subconscious mind will work toward making them occur at the pre-determined time.

Like NLP, unless you want to devote the time and money necessary to become a professional in this area, I suggest employing the services of a trained professional to help you with your own, personal goals. The services of a trained NLP and/or Time Line Therapy® practitioner may seem expensive, but the dramatic and rapid results they can provide should prove to be more than worth the cost.

9. Pray. If you are a praying person, you may consider changing the way you pray. Do you pray with faith? Think about it. Are you really praying like you believe you already have the thing you're praying for? Many people aren't. Start thanking God that you already (fill in the blank), instead of begging in such a desperate, needy way that it reinforces your lack of what you want instead of strengthening your faith that you already have it. Positive beliefs can easily be phrased as thank you prayers to God.

10. Leave yourself notes, cards, voice messages—whatever. Use your imagination. Find new ways to flood your mind with the positive beliefs you want in your subconscious. Use so many ways at the same time that there is no possible way for the negative beliefs to stay—there's just no room for them.

There are plenty of things you can do to reprogram your subconscious and install what you want in there while getting rid of what you don't want in there. Just remember that if you really want dramatic change, you need to be willing to take dramatic steps to get that change. Stop hanging out with negative people; don't expose your mind to negativity; most of all, keep a constant supply of positive thoughts entering your mind as much as possible.

And don't forget to, whenever possible, combine the words and thoughts with visualization and the emotions associated with presently being, doing, or having what you desire.

Here's a suggestion. Put yourself on a thirty, sixty or ninety-day program of dramatic change. Create a "thinking program" for yourself. Plan out how you're going to avoid allowing negative thoughts to enter your mind and how you're going to replace negative thoughts that do come into your mind with pre-planned positive thoughts designed to push the negative ones out. Decide on how you're going to flood your mind with the positive core beliefs that you want to program into your subconscious. I suggest writing this out.

Do this with only the core positive beliefs you want to program into your subconscious—no specific goals just yet. Flood your mind in every way you can think of so that you will start to believe more positive things about yourself and your ability to become successful.

After you notice those new core beliefs taking root and starting to have an effect on your thinking, then start getting specific with your goals and use the process in this book to achieve any goal you decide to pursue. Achieving goals will become natural. You will expect success, not failure. Your subconscious goal-seeking machine will be working toward your success, not your failure.

You will probably find, after you start working on specific goals, that it will still be a good idea to continue with some belief reprogramming, so you may have some of both things going on at the same time. That's perfectly fine, of course. The main things to remember are that you need to program your beliefs to not conflict with your goals, and don't try to do too much at once.

You will find over time that meeting certain goals will also assist in reprogramming your beliefs about yourself, so both of these things can work together. I only suggest reprogramming your beliefs first because if you don't, you are likely to have much more difficulty realizing your goals.

In fact, this is probably the reason that most people get distracted and simply forget about following through with their goal-achievement strategy—their subconscious is programmed to sabotage this effort. At the very least, it's not programmed to support this effort.

Once you find your groove, so to speak, you will probably be reprogramming certain beliefs about yourself and working toward goals compatible with your new chosen beliefs at the same time. Once you get good at this, there will be no stopping you from creating the life that *you* decide you want.

Achieving Your Goals

Remember that Jesus said you will have what you ask if you believe that you have already received it. (Mark 11:24 NIRV) So, here's the big question. How can you believe you have something that you apparently do not have?

Well, it helps a lot if you have gone through the process before and know firsthand that it works. Because if you know firsthand that the process works, you will realize that you actually *do* have what it is you want, once you begin the process. There's just a delay in its arrival.

For example, let's say that you've been looking for a particular item that you very much want to buy. You found it online and you place your order. You know with certainty that the item is yours—you just purchased it. But you also realize that it will take a week or two to arrive in the mail.

That's the kind of faith or belief you have to have for this to work. And after you've tried it a few times successfully, it gets a lot easier to believe in the process.

For example, I've ordered books many times from Amazon.com. They've always arrived. If I place an order, I fully expect my order to arrive within a reasonable period of time. Once I place my order, the book is mine—even though it hasn't arrived yet.

That's how faith works. You start the process (place your order), then you believe that you have already received what you asked for—it's on its way. Then you feel gratitude, not lack. (The feeling of gratitude will attract more good things into your life—the feeling of lack will repel them.)

So, what is the process? Well, I'm just a mortal—certainly not God, but I have written out a process that I have found to work. I integrated the things I listed earlier, that move you toward a goal, into steps to effectively believe and receive what you desire. Here are the steps:

1. Decide and Focus

2. Speak

3. Visualize

4. Experience Emotions

5. Take Action

Decide and Focus

If you want to be, do, or have any particular thing, you need to decide very specifically what that thing is. You must clearly define it and focus on it—do not allow yourself to be distracted by things that are not it or by a fuzzy image or definition of it.

Don't try to go for too many things at once either. That will ruin your focus and dilute your effectiveness.

The smaller the number of things you're trying to accomplish at the same time, the better your focus will be. Leave some things for later.

Speak

This is very important. Watch what you say. When you talk about this thing you want to be, do, or have, do you talk about it like it is in your present? Do you have a calm confidence that it now exists in your life? Or do you talk about it like it eludes you? Do you seem frustrated from the lack of this thing, or happy because you already have it?

Write out some positive statements that put this thing in the present and memorize them.

To create an easy example, let's just say that you want to buy a house and you need $10,000 to put down. Do you talk about this as if you're frustrated for not having it? Or do you say something like, "I'm getting closer and closer to having my $10,000 down payment every day—the rest of it is on its way to me right now."?

Lie to Yourself!

That's right. Most people lie to themselves anyway—placing unnecessary limitations on their lives by making negative statements that are only true because they keep repeating them.

If you're going to lie to yourself, do it in such a way as to create something good for yourself instead of something bad. Say things like, "I'm getting younger, richer, and better looking every day." The things you say about yourself point you in that direction. Choose the direction you want to move toward and talk like it's in your present.

Visualize

Like the first two items on this list, doing this effectively is a skill that takes practice to develop. Keeping in mind that we need to believe that we have already received what we want, we have to see it. And we can see it in our minds. "For as he thinketh in his heart, so is he (Proverbs 23:7, KJV)."

In addition to drafting statements to speak out loud, we need to create pictures of ourselves in the situation we desire to be in. More effective still is a mental video clip. Create a thirty- to sixty-second mental video clip of yourself in the situation that you desire. Not seeing yourself from a different perspective—but seeing through your own eyes. Play this clip back in your mind every day, while in a calm "state of suggestibility" (alpha state).

Experience Emotions

While you're repeating your positive statements and playing back your mental video clip, make sure that you are truly imagining yourself in that situation. Take the time to experience the emotions you would feel if you were actually in that situation in real time.

The first time I did this exercise, I was actually surprised at which emotions I felt. I thought I would feel excitement and exhilaration. Instead, I felt relief. I felt relaxed and like I could finally let go of the stress that I didn't even realize I had been carrying around with me for so long.

You may also be surprised at the emotions you'll experience when you do this. But doing this exercise will help you to create what you want, attract it to you, attract yourself to it, and start believing that you already have what you desire.

Take Action

I almost didn't add this step because it should be automatic. For many of us, we have been taking action so hard for so long that what we really need to do is relax and go through the mental aspect of all this and stop worrying so much about taking action. The fact is, the actions we've taken have not been effective anyway.

However, in most cases, we will still need to take action. We just need to change how we take action and change which actions we take. Instead of taking the actions that we've always taken in the past, we need to go through the other steps first and then let our subconscious guide us to the actions that will be effective.

Remember that the subconscious mind is a goal-seeking machine. It wants what it's programmed to want—whether that's what we want consciously or not. And our subconscious always goes after what it wants. It believes and it obeys orders. That's why we've made so many stupid decisions in the past. Somehow our subconscious got programmed to want something contradictory to what we want consciously.

That's how someone becomes their own worst enemy. That's why so many of us have had self-defeating behaviors. If you have experienced a pattern of *not* getting what you want out of life, you must accept the fact that your subconscious was programmed to seek something contrary to what you want consciously.

And your subconscious is generally much more powerful and effective at getting what it wants than your conscious mind is. That's why you must reprogram the subconscious if you want to be, do, and have what will make you the most happy, fulfilled person that you can possibly be.

So, instead of continuing to take action like you have up to this point, if you want your results to change, you have to change the things you do that produce results. If you change the cause, you change the effect. Once you get your subconscious on board with what you want consciously, your automatic goal-seeking machine will work for you, not against you. Then you will put the right causes into action, which will change your effects.

What this means, as far as your taking action goes, is that you will feel inclined to take different and more effective actions. Your judgment will serve you better. Your gut instincts will point you in better directions. Your decisions will cause more desirable results. Your self-defeating behaviors will melt away. You will create a magnetic force between yourself and what you want, and your actions will pull your goals closer to you and push you closer to your goals.

Now, let's put these steps together in a theoretical example of how this process can work to change someone's life.

Let's say that John Doe is a forty-plus-year-old man stuck in a dead-end job, who's getting frustrated because even though he gets paid enough to support his family, he's not getting ahead, doesn't enjoy his job, and he's wondering how he's ever going to be able to retire.

To make matters worse, he sees co-workers who he believes to be less deserving passing him up through promotions, just because they have college degrees and he was never "able" to finish his. There is a position within the company that pays significantly more than he earns now, and he's sure he would enjoy that position much more than his present one. The only problem is that this position requires a four-year degree, which he never finished.

He is frustrated, of course, but he doesn't see any way to change the situation he's in. Every time he thinks about it, he just gets more frustrated, because he knows he could be successful in that position. But he's also sure that there's no way he could ever go back to college and finish his degree. His credits are too old, he can't afford the tuition, and he's already too tired when he gets home from work to even think about studying or taking classes. Whatever energy he can come up with in the evening goes to doing things with the kids or occasionally even spending a little time with his also tired wife.

Somehow or another, John Doe's subconscious got programmed to believe that he can't go back to school and finish his degree. He's like the elephant that can't pull the little wooden stake out of the grass.

The answer could be so obvious as to be staring John right in the face, and he wouldn't be able to see it because he's so convinced that his situation is impossible. But let's go further in the example.

Let's say that in spite of his previous programming, which is causing him to believe that he's stuck in an impossible situation, John happens to listen to some presentation, sermon, whatever—where someone gets him thinking about possibilities and that "it's never too late to be who you might have been." (George Eliot)

For the first time in years, John allows himself to think about the possibility that he can rise above his current situation. He goes home and asks his wife what she thinks, and she is surprisingly supportive. (In fact, she's been wishing he had done this a long time ago.) Now that he accepts the possibility that it could happen, let's say that he starts to desire this as a reality in his life. But he has no idea how it could possibly happen.

Even though he has no idea how it could happen, let's say that John is at least imagining what his life could be like if he did finish that degree and got a promotion.

While we're at it, let's say that now that he's started to shift the way he's thinking just a little bit, he notices the book on his night stand that a friend had lent to him earlier but that he had been ignoring because he was thinking negatively and, therefore, repelling good things instead of attracting them.

It's this book, of course. (I have to get these instructions in front of him somehow for our example in order to show how the process works.) John starts reading this book and decides to try out the five-step process to making something good happen in his life.

Step 1—Decide and Focus: John thinks about what he wants and he makes a decision. Instead of a whole bunch of conflicting goals, he chooses one thing to focus on and make his goal. He can do this with other things later on, but he decides on this one thing to start. His goal is to finish the bachelor's degree he started around twenty years ago. He still has no idea how he will do it. But he has completed Step #1. (He wrote it down, by the way.)

Step 2—Speak: He drafted a written statement to memorize and keep in his mind as he goes about his day. His statement was, "I am an educated professional, and I am proud to have earned my bachelor's degree." He still doesn't have any idea how he's going to do it, but he's following the steps, so he repeats this statement often and thinks about it throughout the day.

Step 3—Visualize: In his imagination, John put together a 1-minute video clip, which he plays back in his mind several times every evening while he's drifting off to sleep. He imagines getting up in the morning, happier and more satisfied with his life than he was before, putting on nicer clothes than he did before, driving to work in a nicer vehicle than he did before, being greeted with more respect than he was before, enjoying his job more than he did before, getting a bigger paycheck than he did before, and driving back home to a larger and fancier home than he did before, to be greeted by a family who appears to be happier and more impressed by him than they were before. (He still doesn't know how he's going to do it.)

Step 4—Experience Emotions: While John repeats his drafted phrase or watches his mental video clip, John pays special attention to making sure that he experiences the exact same emotions that he would feel if he were actually there in that situation. He notices that he feels more relaxed, more confident, happier, more positive, more fulfilled and more satisfied. He has energy left over to pay more attention to his wife and kids. He doesn't worry about money so much, so he can enjoy his time with his family more. John takes the time to experience the emotions and enjoy what it feels like to be in the position he wants to be in.

He still has no idea how he's going to pull it off, but now he has more conscious desire than ever to make this a reality. Now that John is vividly imagining himself in that situation and experiencing the emotions associated with it, he's starting to send a signal to his subconscious mind that it may be receiving some new orders that must be carried out.

Step 5—Take Action: As John goes through these steps and consistently imagines himself in the position he wants to be in, his subconscious mind starts to accept this imagined situation as its new set of orders that must be obeyed.

Therefore, his subconscious is working out the details, doing the planning and generally figuring out how to go about completing this task. John starts getting new ideas and inspiration as to how this thing might actually be able to become a reality. He even starts to find himself believing that it can happen. He finds it easier and easier to believe that he has already received what he wants when the new ideas start popping into his mind as to how he could actually fulfill this objective.

As he starts to think positively about his new situation instead of negatively about his old situation and starts thinking of ideas as to how he could actually achieve this goal, he becomes motivated naturally to take action. Being able to see the results in his mind, as if they've already taken place, makes John very motivated, indeed. He doesn't need to force himself to do something he dreads and doesn't believe to be possible; he feels naturally motivated—he actually *wants* to take the actions he is imagining.

He notices, for example, that he stays up an hour later every night than he needs to, watching TV to relax. He could actually go to sleep an hour earlier every night, get up an hour before the rest of his family every morning, and get an hour of uninterrupted study time before he gets ready for work.

He also happens to be listening this time when someone mentions the employee tuition reimbursement program, which would cover the costs of finishing his degree. Then he looks online and discovers that there's an accredited school in his area that will let him study and test out of certain things he may have already studied a long time ago and that it has a class schedule that would work for him and his family so that he can take the classes he needs. It even has an online option that is very flexible and would work with his schedule.

It turns out that John can finish his degree in about eighteen months of part-time study, and with his experience, he'll be a shoe-in for the next promotion available. Now, John is able to start seeing this goal as something that is sure to be completed if he just takes the actions that he now knows that he is able to take. He has the motivation and knows what to do, so it becomes a very natural thing to start taking the actions required to meet his goal.

Once John is off and running with this goal, he may set another one. The next goal will be easier to believe in now that he knows the process works. Next time, it's easier to believe that once he's done Step 1—decided exactly and clearly what the goal is—it's already on its way to him; he only needs to continue the process through the other steps. In other words, he can believe that he's already received what he wants—and therefore, it will become reality.

Our John Doe example is only one of many scenarios that would be very easy to think of. The important thing to you is thinking of one for yourself. What do you want to be, do, or have? Can you think of one single thing that you can decide on to put into the system and see what happens? If you have success with that first thing, do you think you could start to believe that as soon as you decide on and clearly define a goal, you've already received it—because you put it into the system, and it's on it's way to you as if it's "in the mail?"

After doing this a few times, you will develop the skill of putting your desire "into the system" and knowing what the result will be. When you can believe 100 percent that the result is already yours—because you put your desire "into the system" and you know what happens when you do that—you will *know* that the thing is yours, before it actually arrives. Then the scripture becomes real and rational to you. Ask, believing that you have already received it—and it will be yours.

Section 3: A Few Interesting Concepts, Ideas, etc.

There are a number of ideas that are good to be aware of if your goal is to reprogram your subconscious mind for success. We'll hit on a few of them here.

From Elephant to Bumblebee

In the previous example, I mentioned that John Doe was like the elephant that couldn't pull the little wooden stake out of the grass. In other words, there was something he couldn't do, simply because his subconscious mind wouldn't let him—because he was programmed to believe that he could not do it. Somehow, John's subconscious mind received a message that it interpreted to be an order it must obey or a status it must protect. He was, therefore, incapable of doing that thing – not because it wasn't possible, but simply due to the incredible power of subconscious programming.

The circus elephant is a perfect example of this. When he was born, this baby elephant was chained to a heavy iron stake, which was buried deep in the ground. The elephant fought and fought until it simply gave into the fact that there was no way it could get loose.

Once the elephant was programmed to believe that it was incapable of getting loose, they could then take that elephant anywhere, secured by nothing more than a small wooden stake pushed into the grass only a few inches. Now a full-grown elephant, it could pull that wooden stake out of the ground as easily as you or I could lift a paper napkin. But it is limited by what it believes about itself. It actually cannot pull loose—but only because it's so sure that it cannot.

Compare that with the bumblebee. Aerodynamically, the bumblebee cannot fly. At least, that's what a certain scientist determined a few years ago. But don't try to convince the bumblebee. It knows it can fly—because it saw other bumblebees flying and there was no one there to teach it that it could not fly. In fact, it was only because bumblebees do fly that more recent scientists were able to study them and eventually figure out exactly what they do that allows them to fly. Often, it is only because someone accomplishes "the impossible" that we discover what really is possible.

John Doe needed to go from elephant to bumblebee. How about you? Have you been holding yourself back, simply because of what you were programmed to believe about yourself? What would happen if you were to reprogram your subconscious so effectively that you could be more like the bumblebee than the elephant? Imagine what your life would be like if you were to stop placing unnecessary limitations on yourself, and instead, be able to start doing things that those around you might even have believed to be impossible – until they saw you do it.

You might consider taking a few minutes right now to imagine the possibilities. While you're at it, insert pictures and experience emotions. This might inspire you to reach a new goal that you would never have attempted otherwise. Remember what Henry Ford said, "Whether you think you can, or you think you can't—you're right."

Do the Opposite

I'm a huge *Seinfeld* fan. If you're very young or you just moved here from another planet, this was a great television sitcom starring Jerry Seinfeld and arguably the best sitcom ever put on television. It's amazing what you can learn from unlikely sources like this.

In one of the episodes, Jerry told George that if every single instinct he had was wrong, the opposite would have to be right. So George started doing the exact opposite of what he felt inclined to do in any given situation and things completely turned around for him. It was actually quite hilarious.

This was obviously fiction and was not supposed to be realistic. But there is some degree of truth in that idea. If we were programmed for failure—and we can answer that question simply by looking at our long-term results so far—what we consider to be our gut reactions, our instincts, our decision-making process, what we feel would be the best reaction or decision in a given situation, will probably be wrong a good deal of the time.

Remember that if you're not where you want to be in life and you really have tried, then the instincts, judgment, etc. that you have exercised to this point has been wrong a good deal of the time. Otherwise, things would have worked out better because your decisions would have been better. Your subconscious is working against you by trying to carry out what it perceives to be strict orders based on erroneous and destructive information.

The idea of doing the opposite of what your gut instincts tell you to do is not to be taken 100 percent seriously, of course. Some instincts will still be correct. You obviously don't want to do stupid things just because you *don't* think you should.

But it is important to realize that perhaps the decisions you have made in the past were wrong and that they were wrong because of bad subconscious programming. Therefore, your gut reactions cannot always be trusted until your subconscious has been reprogrammed.

For example, let's say that one of your self-defeating behaviors is getting frustrated with a job and quitting it. Suppose that something comes up in your job and you find yourself in such a frustrating position that you can't imagine staying there any longer. Someone has been offering you an alternative, and it looks like it's time to take it.

Well, if you've had that decision-making pattern for a few years and your career is not where you had hoped it would be, perhaps it's time to "do the opposite." Making a conscious decision to go contrary to your subconscious programming is one way to get a different result. Maybe by sticking out the situation, you'll find that it improves with a little more time and that by being there longer, you'll learn how to be more successful at that job, get promotions, benefit from good times as well as enduring down times, etc.

The point is that if you can identify some of the ways that you were programmed counterproductively and some of the ways you tend to act, react, or make decisions; you can then identify what to do differently. As you start to experience different results, you will learn more about the cause-and-effect relationships in your life, and you'll be able to see more clearly what has been causing your life to be different than you wanted it to be.

Doing "the opposite" alone is probably not going to be sufficient because our subconscious programming is very strong and often hard to identify, but this is one thing that you can do to change your direction.

Remember that if it's subconscious programming you're battling, you have to realize that what you feel in your gut would be the best decision may very well be the wrong one—because your gut was programmed to sabotage you, at least in some ways—not to help you.

My entire life, I have carefully thought things through and tried to make wise decisions. I've studied, weighed out both sides, investigated options, prayed, consulted people I trusted, listened to my heart, etc., and guess what. I made a lot of bad decisions that put my life in the wrong direction for a long time.

The fact is, whether we're talking about gut reactions, good feelings about something, perceived inspiration, or logical and calculated decisions based on all the available facts—if your subconscious was programmed to sabotage you, it is capable of using all these avenues to do so.

You need to reprogram your subconscious—and do some things contrary to your subconscious programming until you've been able to reprogram adequately.

I tried this myself a little while back, with an issue that I had been dealing with, and "doing the opposite" from what my gut instincts (subconscious programming) tried to persuade me to do actually resulted in a significant success for me. And making the decision to go against the negative programming of the past, and having that decision work out for me, actually helped me to reprogram myself in that area.

If you do decide to "do the opposite" for a certain situation, just make sure you're doing it for a reason—namely, that the way you have reacted to a certain situation in the past proved to be the wrong choice after the fact, and you don't want to repeat those results.

Once you've sufficiently reprogrammed your subconscious mind to stop sabotaging your life, doing "the opposite" should no longer be necessary. Then you can go back to trusting your instincts and your decisions will be much better than they were before.

Fear versus Faith

We've all read about, or at least heard of, the incredible things that have been accomplished by faith. The process that I detailed of how to achieve your goals is actually the process of exercising faith, the way I choose to illustrate it, at least.

We were basically programmed to do things backwards. We want to receive something physically before believing that we have it. But that approach is exactly the opposite of how to get what you want. Remember what Jesus said about asking, believing that you've already received. We have to receive it in our minds, or hearts, first—it arrives physically afterwards.

Okay—so we've actually spent a good deal of time talking about faith. Now, let's talk about fear. Fear is the opposite of faith. Put another way, fear is exercising faith in something that you do *not* want to happen.

Think about this for a minute. Let's say that you're a real estate agent, for example, during a very difficult market. Let's say that you haven't made a sale in a while and you're almost out of money. You start to dwell on what will happen if you don't get money right away. You imagine the utilities getting shut off and having no money for food. You start to panic, wondering how you're going to live if you don't get X number of dollars by Y date and thinking that it is not even possible to get X dollars by Y date.

You're picturing and experiencing the emotions of already having accomplished that horrible situation—but you're doing it in the comfort of your warm home while having something to eat! It hasn't happened yet! But in your mind, you're already living it! You are exercising faith in what you do *not* want to happen. And it's easy to do, isn't it? What if you were as good at exercising faith in something that you actually want to happen?

Believe me, I know what I'm talking about here. I was a pro at this. I had to make this part of my personal reprogramming project. When this happens, we have to be prepared to fight this. We need weapons and ammunition. We need a battle plan.

Part of my mental rehab program was to flood my mind with positive, can-do thoughts—to put so much positive stuff in my mind and with such force that it pushes out all the negative programming that's been in there for so long.

One of the things I did was to watch a Joel Osteen DVD every morning during breakfast instead of watching the "bad news" on TV. In fact, I still try to do that. And he's not paying me to say this.

You pick what works for you—but be armed for the fight with something—lots of things: Bible verses, DVDs, sayings that you memorize, pictures of what you want, memories of situations that looked bad but worked out for the best—everything you can get your hands on.

When fear comes after you, you send it running like chickens from a wolf. You turn on it with a ferocity that knows no limits. If you let fear take from you what is rightfully yours, you're a loser. If you control fear, turn your thoughts to faith that you are getting what you want, and then achieve what you're after—you're a winner.

Rico's Rules for Dealing with Challenges

When you find yourself reacting negatively to a situation, you need to replace those negative thoughts and emotions with positive ones. Remember that the emotions you currently associate with a given issue will give you a pretty good idea of what you're attracting and what you're repelling. You need to keep your emotions positive and constructive as much as possible in order to attract positive results to any given situation.

Here are four things to keep in mind. In fact, it may be a good idea to memorize these and say them out loud to yourself over and over again, thinking about what they really mean. This can help you to start thinking and feeling the positive, optimistic attitude that you need to point yourself in the right direction. On numerous occasions, I have completely changed my mood within two minutes, simply by reminding myself of these four rules:

Rule #1: God can fix anything.

Rule #2: Every negative can be turned into a positive.

Rule #3: What you visualize and speak *will* become reality.

Rule #4: It's all part of the adventure, baby!

Let's talk about these individually.

#1—God can fix anything.

I realize that there are a lot of different types of people reading this book, and I'm not trying to impose my religious views onto anyone. But if you do believe in an all-powerful God, believing that He can fix anything is probably not too much of a stretch for you.

One of the ways we can find peace in this world is to trust that God is with us, knows what we need better than we do, and has better solutions for us than we may have. There is a peace in trusting in God, and if we're going to trust in God, we should do it in the midst of challenges—not only when things are just right.

When things aren't quite what we want them to be, if we can relax a little and trust that God is with us and knows what we need and that He really does want what's best for us, this can help us to stop worrying and start thinking more positively. It helps sometimes just to remind ourselves that God really can fix anything.

#2—Every negative can be turned into a positive

I believe that there is a natural law of the universe that, once we understand it, can be a huge help to our attitude and our circumstances when something is not how we want it to be.

Basically, this spiritual law says that when something happens, if it is negative, it can be made to be positive—at least to the magnitude that it was negative. And (Rico's corollary) if thrust into positive territory with enough force, it can be made to be a positive with even greater magnitude than it was a negative.

First of all—and this is very important—we don't even know initially whether some things are negative or positive. We are not aware of all factors at play at any given time, and we are certainly not able to see into the future, so we really can't judge whether everything that happens is inherently negative or positive to us until we have the full context of how that specific piece fits into the larger puzzle.

Read and pronounce the following words: *live* and *read*. Did you pronounce the first word to rhyme with *give* or with *dive*? Did you pronounce the second one to rhyme with *deed* or with *head*? That's right—you don't know which word I intended because you don't have any context.

Suppose I ask you to pronounce these same two words when I put them in a sentence, like this: "If you will *read* these words and *live* by them, you will succeed." In context, it is easy to know how to pronounce these two words, but out of context, you're not really sure.

The same applies when something happens to you in life. Let's take an example. Suppose you are in outside sales and you meet prospective customers at their respective places of business and you set up your appointments in advance in order to operate efficiently.

On one day, you travel across town to make a fifty thousand dollar sale that you had every reason to believe was already a done deal. The appointment stood you up, and the person who was there informed you that the prospect already purchased from someone else. A "normal" person would naturally assume that what just happened was a negative event. But that is because we generally seem to think the wrong way. A real winner will look for a way to turn that "negative" event into a positive one.

Perhaps this client was going to turn out to be a real pain in the you-know-what. Perhaps you hear later that there was a horrible traffic accident that you would most likely have been involved in had you finished that appointment and left at the anticipated time. The fact is, there may be a hundred possible reasons—that you can't see—why this could actually have been a positive occurrence and not a negative one, as you might have assumed.

In addition, since there is always a way to turn something "negative" into something positive, it is now your job to stop and say, "Okay. Now what can I do to make this seemingly negative situation into a positive one?" Perhaps there is another prospect in that area that you have not been able to reach by phone. Maybe you drive or walk over there, catch that person at just the right time, and go back to your office with a one hundred thousand dollar sale instead of a fifty thousand dollar sale. You have then turned a potentially negative situation into a positive one.

It's easy to get frustrated when it appears that something negative has happened. I know this well—I was quite talented at getting frustrated when things "go wrong." Evidently, that was part of my loser programming. And part of making the transformation from loser to winner is the belief that you can create good in some way or another from anything that happens. When something happens, don't just assume that it is a negative thing; look for a way to turn this event into a positive of equal or greater magnitude.

Lest someone misunderstand my thinking, I should clarify something. Sometimes something so unspeakably awful happens to us or someone we love, that it seems horribly inappropriate to think to ourselves, "Hm...so-and-so just died a horrible death. How can I turn this event to my advantage?" This is, of course, not what I am trying to teach here.

But many times, in the face of very trying circumstances, a person rises out of the ashes to become a stronger or a better person. These awful events that no one wants can actually serve to reveal, develop, and strengthen our character and make us into the people that we can and should become. That doesn't mean that you will ever be glad that a certain event occurred; it simply means that the potential benefit that comes through this experience is realized.

Other times, something horrible can happen to a person and that person allows it to ruin his or her life. How we react to things shapes our character, our personality, and our lives.

And when something does happen—that we would never want to happen—we still have the choice as to how we will react to that circumstance. It may be one of those types of events that we could never look back on and be happy that it occurred, but we can still come out of it having obtained some benefit or having grown in some way, as opposed to letting the event ruin us.

Traumatic events can get past your mental filter and into your subconscious mind. And your brain can distort the memories in the process. If you can program your subconscious brain to take on challenges with optimism and a healthy, winning attitude, you reduce the likelihood that a traumatic event will scar you for life, and you increase the growth aspect of living through these things that nobody ever looks forward to.

Many things simply weren't as bad as we thought they were when they happened. Many things that we initially thought were negative turned out to be positive, without any specific intervention on our part. Other things that happened may have been those types of events that were initially negative, but that carried with them the opportunity to be transformed into something positive and are the types of situations where we can actually wind up being glad that they happened—if we respond to them positively instead of reacting to them negatively.

Then, of course, there are those awful things that we feel no one should ever have to endure. These are the things that are so bad, we could never be glad that they happened. But keep in mind that even these things require a certain type of response if you are going to be a winner instead of a loser. You can still grieve, and you should. You can still feel that it was an awful event that never should have happened—and you are probably right. But you can still have an overall reaction over time that causes some significant benefit to yourself or someone else because this horrible event occurred.

Think of John Walsh of the television show *America's Most Wanted*. In 1981, John's son, Adam, was abducted and murdered by a convicted sex offender. The man who confessed to this crime died in prison while serving a life sentence for other crimes (Biography.com). Mr. Walsh didn't even get the satisfaction of seeing this perverted criminal punished for this particular crime. I'm quite certain that, no matter what he does, Mr. Walsh will never be happy that this horrible event occurred.

But it did occur, and John Walsh appears to be a winner, not a loser. So, how did he react? Well, I'm sure that he felt horrible and grieved appropriately. I am sure he was angry and wanted justice. But he didn't stop there. He did something that he probably would not have done otherwise that made a huge difference to others.

As a result of that horrible event, we saw the development of the Adam Walsh Child Resource Center, The Adam Walsh Child Protection and Safety Act, "Code Adam," and, of course, the Fox television show *America's Most Wanted*. As a result of the TV show, well over 1,000 criminals have been caught—so far. Imagine how many crimes may have been prevented due to the capture of over one thousand criminals on the loose. Walsh has also helped to bring home over fifty missing children. Though John Walsh will certainly never be happy about what happened, he clearly used this event in a positive way and has made a significant difference in the lives of many grateful people.

Most often, the things that happen that we feel are negatives are not nearly this serious. And many of those were not really negatives to begin with, if we looked at them the right way. But what we really need to do is to develop the kind of character that habitually turns negatives into positives and that meets challenges with the resolve of a winner mentality.

Because it can, upon occasion, be difficult to find exactly the best way to turn a negative into a positive, here's a way to make sure that you're never without a solution.

If something "bad" happens and you want to turn the negative into a positive, if you can't find what you would consider to be the best way to do that, remember this. The two things don't necessarily have to be related! Just pick something that you wouldn't have done otherwise.

For example, let's say that you had an unexpected expense that you consider to be significant and that you will not really get anything beyond status quo for this unexpected loss of money. The transmission goes out on your car—something like that. It's an expense, but you get nothing new for it—just the same car working as it did before.

Suppose that you have been unable to find some way to turn that negative into a positive. Well, just pick something that you wouldn't have done otherwise that can make you twice as much money as the new transmission just cost you. Perhaps you decide to call on a few new prospective customers that you would not have—until you earn an extra amount of income that doubles the unexpected expense.

Maybe you brainstorm and find a better, more efficient, or more profitable way to do something in your business. It doesn't have to be related to the transmission—it only has to be something you weren't planning to do before the transmission went out, that will benefit you more than the "bad news" hurt you.

Thinking along these lines whenever a "negative" event occurs will help you to take control of your circumstances and get the results you want out of life, instead of feeling like a victim of circumstances beyond your control. It will help you to go from loser to winner.

Once enough things start to go right instead of wrong, you may not want to bother messing with every annoying thing that comes up—not everything has to go exactly right for you to have a great life. You may decide to just let some things go. But using this technique will certainly help you get to the point where you feel like you can do that without letting things bother you so much—and you'll know it's always there if you need it. Once you've gotten some practice in, a good rule of thumb is: if it really bothers you—use the technique. If not, just let it go and focus on something positive.

#3—What you visualize and speak *will* become reality.

We talked about this so much already that we really don't need to elaborate more here. It's just good to remind yourself of this when you're thinking of the "Rules." It really can help to change your attitude quickly when you're tempted to become frustrated over something.

#4—It's all part of the adventure, baby!

Lighten up a little, will you? This life was never supposed to be a tiptoe through the tulips every single day of our time here. Helen Keller said, "Life is either a daring adventure or nothing." We need to remember and keep the attitude that this life is our very own personal adventure. An interesting story that we write with every decision we make. It has drama, suspense, tragedy, romance, humor, action, and, hopefully, it ends with a great victory.

But there may be challenges that have to be overcome. That's one of the things that can make our story so interesting and our life so fulfilling. When we take on a challenge and we become victors over our difficulties, we earn a sense of fulfillment that we can't get any other way. It's just like a movie being interesting because of the challenges that the movie star had to overcome.

Get excited about your adventure! Remember what it felt like to be young and excited about getting out into the world and starting your adult life—believing that you could be, do, and have anything and everything you wanted. Do you remember that optimistic feeling you had before life beat you down?

Well, now you have the secret to being able to get that feeling and attitude back. You know what to do to achieve the life you've always wanted. And if you've had some challenges along the way, now is the time to rise up and attack life with a renewed energy and enthusiasm and a new confidence that you can achieve what you want out of life—in spite of everything that's happened the wrong way. Make this story fun and interesting! Make the movie of your life something you can be proud of—it's completely up to you.

Do you remember the movie *The Game*, starring Michael Douglas and Sean Penn? Michael Douglas played a character who had it all, but evidently, Sean Penn's character thought that Douglas's character had no adventure in his life. Penn's character paid an exorbitant amount of money to set up a situation where Douglas's character had to experience some very intense moments—and he believed it all to be real. Seemingly life-threatening, scary stuff—nothing anyone would ever want to go through. But it created an adventure for him, and it made his predictable life more interesting.

I don't believe that we need to go out of our way to bring problems into our lives just so we can solve them—life has a way of naturally presenting things to us for us to deal with. Let's just enjoy our adventure and live life to its fullest. Let's live so that one day, when we're looking back on our adventure, we smile and feel a sense of fulfillment, not regret.

I suggest that next time you get frustrated by something that happens that you didn't want to happen, you pull out an index card and read aloud, "One: God can fix anything. Two: every negative can be turned into a positive. Three: what you visualize and speak *will* become reality. Four: it's all part of the adventure, baby!" Think about what these things mean to you. Your whole attitude will change almost instantly.

Don't Just Do Something—Be Something!

There's a reason that I put achievements into the three categories of *be*, *do*, and *have*. I think this is what makes our lives. Who and what do we want to be? What do we want to do? What do we want to have? Instead of the usual categories everyone else has already used, I wanted to separate things this way because I think it helps define who we are and what kind of adventure we're having on this planet.

This part might not apply quite as much for some of you ladies (though it will for others), but I know that at least for us men, we get a very large part of our identity, self-esteem, and perception of our value from what we do for a living. When a man meets anyone for the first time, it's invariably one of the first questions or topics for small talk that comes up.

To a great extent, a man is defined, categorized, and his value judged by what he does to earn money—or what he did to earn his wealth if he no longer chooses to work.

Right or wrong, people will find this out before deciding to what extent they should treat a man with respect.

This can be a source of self-confidence or source of embarrassment. Either way, it's a large part of our identity as men. Instead of just doing something to make a living, I believe we really ought to *be* something. We need to decide what we are, and what we want to be.

Some people might say, "It's not who I am; it's just what I do." Of course we don't want to go to extremes here, but my gut reaction to that remark would be, "Then perhaps you should find something that you want to *be*, not just *do*."

How you spend the majority of your waking hours is important. If you spend it doing something you hate, you are wasting a large part of your life. Of course, you might have to do something you hate, or at least would rather not do, for some time in order to be able to feed your family while you're moving into something that you would enjoy more. But it should be an important goal to do something that you don't feel is a waste of your life.

In addition to the fact that you'll be happier spending your time on something that you enjoy rather than on something you don't enjoy, this can be a competitive world, and you will be more likely to put in the time, take the interest, and make the other sacrifices necessary to get really good at something that you like than you will be for something you don't like.

Even though I believe that we should not look at the world as a zero-sum game, where there's not enough to go around; the fact is, if you decide you want a particular type of job and there are many people competing for that type of job, you may have to become quite good at what you do in order to succeed at it. And you're more likely to become really good at what you do if you are interested in that particular thing and find satisfaction in doing it.

Whatever you are doing, there is very likely someone else out there doing something similar, who enjoys it and feels disposed to spend the time required to master it. If it is torture for you to spend time doing this thing and you don't take an interest in increasing your skill or education in that area, you are falling behind someone else who is getting better and better at that thing because they're interested in that thing and it is not torture for them to invest their time and energy into improving their abilities in that area.

Chose a line of work that you can take an interest in. If you are now doing something that you don't like to do, you may have to continue doing it while you're working towards getting into something you'll enjoy. You may even find that it's easiest to build on what you already know, but use that knowledge in a related area. There may be a different position that you could move into, that would utilize your prior education and experience, and it may be something you could enjoy. If so, it may be easier to move into that area than into an area that you have no prior advantages in.

Whether your goal is to work in a specific job for a big company, or to start your own consulting practice helping others in your area of expertise, I suggest that you choose something that you want to *be*, not just something that you want to or think you have to *do*. Then be the best you can be at this thing, and your probability of success—and your level of satisfaction—will skyrocket.

The Attitude of Gratitude

I never really understood the purpose or benefits of gratitude until fairly recently. This is one of those pieces of the puzzle that is often missing from the box for someone who's trying to learn how to be successful.

Just off the top of my head, I can think of several really good reasons to practice gratitude every day.

1. If we want to be blessed, it would behoove us to become closer to the source of those blessings. Sincere gratitude is a very effective way to become closer to God, and the benefits of being closer to God are numerous, indeed.

2. When we focus on what we don't have, we are reinforcing lack in our subconscious minds. When we consistently reinforce lack, it becomes harder to have faith that we will succeed in filling the voids created by the lack.

    Remember that we have to think, picture, speak, and experience the emotions of already having, being, or accomplishing what we desire, if we want these objectives to be realized. When we dwell on what we don't have, we're creating lack, not abundance.

Keeping an "attitude of gratitude" is a great way to reinforce positive results in our lives instead of creating or perpetuating negative results. In addition to dwelling on gratitude for those things that we have already been blessed with, we should also experience gratitude for the things that we desire to be blessed with. Remember that Jesus said we are to ask for what we want, believing that we have already received it.

3. If we're practicing gratitude and we believe that we have already received a certain thing, we will feel gratitude for that thing just like everything else we feel gratitude for—perhaps even more because it is more recent. This gratitude is a very important part of the deliberate process of thinking, speaking, visualizing, and feeling the emotions associated with the fulfillment of a specific goal or desire.

4. When we feel sincere gratitude for the numerous blessings we enjoy, we also feel happier. Not only does this happiness help to attract more blessings into our lives, but this additional happiness we feel as a result of our gratitude also has great value in and of itself. In the big picture, happiness is what we're really trying to achieve, isn't it?

I would like to suggest a different way of looking at things than you may be used to. Most people react to what they perceive to be good or bad in their lives. They feel happy when things are good, and they feel depressed, angry or sad when things are bad.

Here's a better way to look at things. There are always positive and negative things in your life—both happening all around you simultaneously. What you choose to focus on is what you will get more of.

If you look for negative things, you will surely find them. Concentrating on those things and experiencing the accompanying emotions will create a magnetism between you and more negative things.

Choosing to look for positive things, on the other hand, and focusing your attention on these things, and experiencing the emotions that go with dwelling on all the positive things in your life, will create a magnetism between you and more positive things that will now be getting closer and closer to you.

If your foot is on the accelerator, steer the wheel where you want to go—not where you don't want to go. There will always be good and bad happening at the same time. You give the power of proliferation to the one you choose to dwell upon. Choosing to practice the attitude of gratitude every day is a great way to focus on the positive and attract more positive things into your life.

Bless Somebody

Answer this quickly without pondering—if you left a 30 percent tip for a good waiter instead of a 15 to 20 percent tip, did you just waste your money?

Many people believe that if they leave someone a generous tip, they're being irresponsible with their money—wasting it, throwing it away. I'm not suggesting going crazy with this necessarily, but I have an idea for you. This is a way to develop an abundance mentality instead of holding onto a poverty mentality.

Next time you have a good server—someone who merits a good tip—after you calculate your 15 to 20 percent or whatever you consider to be normal, take out an extra few dollars and add it to the tip while thinking to yourself, *I am blessed with an abundant life, and money comes to me naturally. I will enjoy helping another deserving person to also experience abundance. This is money well spent because it is blessing someone else who also deserves it. It will not reduce what I have, because I am always receiving more.* You know, something along those lines.

The point is to stop having a poverty mentality. Think abundance. If you truly believe that your cup is running over, sharing a little with someone else can hardly be considered wasteful, right? This exercise will help you to trade in your poverty mentality for an abundance mentality—and it only costs a few extra bucks that you won't even notice is gone.

Way back when I was a waiter trying to get through school on a very modest income, I remember someone leaving me a tip that was considerably more than the amount of the check. I was working my butt off to stay alive while I was in school, and I can hardly consider it a waste of their money to have left me that generous gift. It is the one tip I still remember after all these years. It was completely unnecessary and very much appreciated.

There are a lot of ways to bless someone. As long as you use good judgment, it is not a waste of money. Not only does this create a positive thing for somebody else, which can have ripple effects and come back to you as well, but it also reinforces an attitude of abundance. It tells your brain that you have more than you need, that you have enough to share. It shows your brain that you expect more to arrive— and more than you need. Your cup runs over.

Forgiveness

You may be wondering what forgiveness has to do with anything. But this can actually have a huge effect on your overall attitude—and on your abundance mentality. It's also great for relationships.

If we are not forgiving, we are holding on to the feeling that we are missing something—or lack something—because of what someone did to us. This is contradictory to the feeling of abundance, that we don't lack anything and that everything we need or want can be easily made available to us. Forgiveness usually benefits the forgiver more than the forgiven.

If you really hold the belief that you are blessed with unlimited abundance, it's easier to forgive others. And remember that what we dwell upon, while experiencing the associated emotions, is what we're going to get more of.

Do you want to relive the hurts of the past—thereby attracting more hurtful things into your life? Or would you prefer to take the attitude that you are blessed with unlimited abundance and the favor of God—and that you have enough in you to be able to forgive someone who has wronged you?

Remember, to forgive does not necessarily mean that you should trust or become vulnerable to this person again. It doesn't even mean that you have to spend time with them. It depends on the situation, of course. But what it really means is that you are willing to release the anger, hurt, and resentment you feel—let it leave you, and allow positive feelings of safety, security, opportunity, health, happiness, prosperity, and love to fill you up—allowing you to attract more of these positive things into your life.

The person doesn't have to apologize—and you may not even tell them they're forgiven. Again, how to handle the situation appropriately depends on the situation. But this forgiveness is really about your attitude of letting go of the negative emotions that hurt you and allowing yourself to experience positive emotions that will benefit you.

By the way, do you want to have a happy marriage? Then do this. Every once in a while—you define the time period—sit down and decide that at this moment, you will now absolutely forgive every single thing that your spouse has ever done to hurt you in any way. Do it whether they agree they did anything wrong or not. Do this together, or do it separately.

If you do this effectively, your attitude toward your spouse will be such that without even noticing, you will treat him or her much more like you did when you first fell in love. And your spouse will respond to that kind of treatment very positively.

So much of what goes wrong in a marriage is simply the way each spouse treats the other on a daily basis, due to resentments they've built up over time. When this happens to you, you probably don't even realize you're not treating each other with love and affection. Or if you do notice, you don't know why, don't care why, don't think it's abnormal, or don't think your spouse deserves any better because of the way he or she has been treating you!

If you will periodically take a few minutes and decide to absolutely forgive every single thing your spouse has ever done to offend or hurt you in any way—and especially if you can get your spouse to do the same—your results will be nothing short of miraculous. And I want to hear about them—please write me with your success stories.

An attitude of forgiveness is much like an attitude of gratitude; it affects your emotions and the way you react to things. It creates magnetism between you and what you want—instead of what you don't want. Best of all, it makes you happy.

While we're talking about forgiveness, realize that it is also important to forgive yourself. This may be the most difficult forgiveness project of all. We have all made mistakes in our past, some mistakes being more serious than others. Certain mistakes can leave us feeling so guilty that subconsciously we cannot accept success because we don't feel worthy of it. We reject the very thing we're seeking, and we don't even realize it.

If you want to have the right programming to be able to receive and enjoy your success, you have to forgive yourself of the sins and errors in your past. Looking back, there may be things you're too ashamed of to even want to think about. But if this is not who you are now, and you have repented and put that behavior behind you, it is time to forgive yourself, to like yourself again, and to allow yourself to have a good life. Don't punish yourself any longer.

This doesn't mean that you're justifying what you've done; it doesn't mean it wasn't wrong; it simply means that your guilty conscience has fulfilled its purpose—it caused you to change your direction and to not repeat the things you feel guilty about. When your feelings of guilt have served their purpose, let them go. Your success, health, and happiness may depend upon it.

Your Mental Thermostat

We talked earlier about the definition of *want* actually being two completely different things, depending on whether we're referring to the conscious or the subconscious mind. We also talked about how most of us generally do things in the wrong order. We expect to have something physically before we have it mentally, whereas the most effective way to actually be, do, or have what we desire is to be, do, or have it mentally first and then watch it materialize afterwards.

I would like to elaborate on this in a slightly different way, in order to help you understand a little better how your subconscious mind actually controls the results you get in life.

Your subconscious is like a thermostat that is programmed with the ability to both heat and cool depending on the current temperature and the settings it's programmed with. There are innumerable possibilities for examples that could be used to illustrate this, but let's use monthly income for our example here.

Let's say that your subconscious mind's "comfort zone" is for you to make $5,000 per month. That's its setting; that's what it "wants," because that's what it perceives to be the orders that it must obey. Somehow or another, the message got sent to your subconscious that this is the proper number, the "right" income, homeostasis, your "normal state", "required state", or "comfort zone."

If you make less than $5,000 per month for whatever reason, your subconscious will find a way to increase your income. If you start to make more than $5,000 per month, your subconscious will find a way to make sure your income goes back down to $5,000. It is only doing its job—to maintain what it believes to be the proper setting.

Now, let's say that you have decided consciously that you desire to earn $10,000 per month. How do you convert your conscious "want" into a subconscious "want"? Just like the thermostat in your home, you will have to reprogram the setting in your subconscious mind, then let your goal-seeking machine do its job. The way you go about doing that is to try to trick your subconscious mind into believing that you already make $10,000 per month.

Now, that said—if you've never received a ten thousand dollar paycheck in your entire life, you know it. But when you go through the proper steps as outlined in this book, you can "believe before receiving" that it is yours.

Attempting to convince your subconscious that you already earn $10,000 per month will reset your mental thermostat so that your subconscious mind will now accept as its normal setting, or comfort zone, that you are supposed to be earning $10,000 per month right now.

Your subconscious will then set out to make the necessary adjustments to create and maintain this status.

When your subconscious mind accepts this new setting as your normal state of being—the state it's supposed to protect—it becomes uncomfortable with any conflicting state. When your subconscious becomes uncomfortable with a state, it sets out to change that state and move your reality into the state it believes to be "normal" for you. Like the thermostat, your subconscious mind will adjust your reality to be consistent with what it was programmed to "want."

And the subconscious always believes that it can do what it thinks it's supposed to do—because it has accepted the programmed state as reality—it believes that this is the state it must maintain. Doubt and fear don't prevent your subconscious from getting what it wants, but these are tools that the subconscious can use—if it's programmed to—to prevent you from getting what you want consciously. That's why we must program the subconscious to *want* what we decide consciously that we really want to achieve.

I want to emphasize this point, even at the risk of sounding redundant and verbose. Your subconscious mind does not look at the programmed state as impossible or improbable—it looks at the programmed state as what is normal for you. It does not doubt its ability to protect this reality; it simply goes about maintaining and protecting what it believes to be the required state. If your current state differs from what the subconscious accepts as the required, or normal, state, it will use all the tools at its disposal to change your current state to conform to its programmed normal state.

What we're talking about here is actually the mechanics of believing before receiving, or exercising faith. You are programming your subconscious desire to be consistent with your conscious desire, thereby creating or growing faith that you have already received what you ask.

When you can consciously choose to have faith in a certain thing because you have learned how to "operate the equipment," as we talked about before—and then program your subconscious mind to believe that the state you want to be in is, in fact, the real and normal state and that any conflicting state is unreal and unacceptable—your subconscious mind will go about its work to seek and protect the status it was programmed to *want*.

Remember that your subconscious mind *wants* to give you what it believes your normal or desired state to be, because it wants to serve you and protect your status quo. It wants to give you what it believes you want, or protect what it believes you have, based on what it was programmed to believe about your "normal" and desired states.

Your conscious and subconscious minds will now agree that you have already received what you ask because the subconscious does not doubt its ability to perform its required tasks. And the results will follow.

When I talk about attempting to convince your mind that it has already received something that it has clearly not yet received, it's not that you have really tricked your mind into believing that you have already received that thing in a literal sense. But the attempt to do so is what reprograms the setting in your subconscious, so that it will accept as its new orders the thing you are trying to achieve or obtain. When you try to convince your subconscious mind that something is already a reality, the subconscious mind's response is to accept this suggested reality as its new orders, or comfort zone. And if any conflicting state exists, that state must be changed to conform to the new required state.

In the example, you will know if you have never gotten a ten thousand dollar paycheck. But if you set out to convince your subconscious mind that you do, in fact, earn $10,000 per month when you have actually only been making $5,000 per month, your subconscious can change the setting for you—it can make your normal state, or comfort zone, a monthly income of $10,000. Now, a lower or higher income than this will be unacceptable, and the subconscious mind will regulate this like the thermostat in your home.

When you change the setting in your subconscious mind, your mind is not really tricked into believing that $5,000 is actually $10,000—it is tricked into believing that if you now make only $5,000, it must make whatever adjustments are necessary for you to start making $10,000. Trying to convince your subconscious that something is already happening now, is the way that you change the setting so that your subconscious will actually make it happen.

Respect the Rules

Don't expect God to operate contrary to the way He set up our universe to function or behave. Even when He does show extreme mercy by providing some kind of miracle we may really need at some point in time, if we want our entire lives to change for the better long term, we have to conform to the way He set up our brains and our universe to function.

We can't get the results we want by trying to operate the equipment in a way contrary to the way it was created to function. God can do whatever He wants—He is God. We are not gods; we must conform to how He created us. He created our brains to work in a certain way. He created the universe to work in a certain way. He is the one who said that we must ask, believing that we have already received what we're asking for. Faith has power in the universe the way God created it. And the more powerful our faith, the better able we are to get the results we want.

Don't Regret It—Fix It

We can all learn a lesson from Warren Buffett. Well, actually we could all learn a few lessons from Warren Buffett, but there is one in particular that I'm referring to.

Warren Buffett is probably the most intelligent, skilled, talented investor of our time. And, though he has seemed to go back and forth with Bill Gates, at one point fairly recently he was reported to be the world's richest man. There is a reason for this, of course.

Though there are many things we could learn from him about investing and finance, there is one thing that I think we can all use. Because of his level of expertise in business management as well as investment analysis, and because of the scale on which he invests, he does something that I don't usually see other investors do. Not to say that no one else ever has, but this is something that I noticed with him, specifically.

Believe it or not, Warren Buffett has not always made every stock pick exactly right. Not to say that his analysis was faulty, but he can't possibly anticipate every little thing that could come up with a company, industry, or the economy. Remember that if we can't see the future, we're making decisions based on incomplete information. Warren Buffett just happens to be highly skilled at making decisions based on incomplete information.

Anyway, the thing I noticed about him is that, at least in some circumstances that I read about, when his pick doesn't work out—he makes it work out! This guy can walk in, take over the management of the company, and make it work! The investment didn't prove profitable because the initial decision was correct—the initial decision worked because he made it work.

That's the attitude we need to have. We don't always have all the information we may need to make the best decision regarding a particular thing. We can't have all the information that could be useful to us because part of that information will only be revealed in the future.

But what we can do is, instead of thinking to ourselves, *Woops, I guess I made the wrong decision,* we can think like Warren Buffett and say to ourselves, *Well, that took an unexpected turn—let's fix it.*

We don't always get the results we want out of a decision because we chose correctly. Oftentimes, we will get the results we want out of a decision because of the way we treat the situation after the decision has been made. The decision proves to be the right one only because we make sure that whatever decision we made actually works.

It may be that the other choice could have worked out more easily than the choice we made. Again, without knowledge of the future, we're making decisions based on partial information. Sometimes we just have to take the decisions we make and make them work.

This is the attitude of a winner—someone who doesn't give up. Someone who makes things happen, instead of someone who watches things happen or who wonders what happened.

Be a Superhero

Now and then, I may suggest looking at something in a certain way only in order to obtain a desired result—not necessarily because the idea should be taken literally. This one can be taken literally only to a certain degree, just not to an unhealthy level—we don't want this to become a disorder.

That said, here's an idea that can help to reprogram your attitude and change your behavior.

Pretend that you're a superhero and your superpower is success. Visualize some power coming down through the ceiling, entering your whole body, and changing the direction of the magnetism of each cell in your body so that all your supercharged cells will work together to create a strong magnetic force between you and whatever it is that you desire to achieve.

Visualize and feel the magnetism and the result of this magnetism. Anything you decide to undertake becomes successful because you're involved. Whatever you touch prospers and succeeds.

Be careful about what you touch, by the way. It is possible to become powerful at accomplishing things that are not worthwhile. Make sure to use your superpowers for good instead of evil.

Your "kryptonite" is negative thought. If you catch yourself allowing negative thoughts to enter your brain, your "powers" become weaker. You must make sure that only positive thoughts are in your brain at all times.

Though this exercise should not be taken too literally, it may be taken a little more literally than many of you might imagine at this point. The fact is, we can create a magnetic force between ourselves and our desires. And we can make this force stronger and stronger until it appears to others to be somewhat of a superpower.

I'm not suggesting trying to leap tall buildings with a single bound—now we're talking disorder—but only that the results different people get can vary widely, depending on how much they have developed their ability to utilize faith, visualization, subconscious reprogramming, etc. When you make the transformation from weak, timid loser, to strong, confident, successful winner—comparatively speaking, you may appear to be a superhero.

Live Your Own Adventure

This life is your very own, personal adventure. If you develop your ability to "believe before you receive" and really master the art and science of creating your own future outcomes, you will have a pretty good idea of how your story ends. At the very least, you will know that at the end of your story, you won.

Now, if that is the case, then you really don't need to be so stressed out about every frustration, inconvenience or setback that occurs along the way, right? I mean, if you know who wins the game, the challenges during the process are what make the game interesting, right? If you know that in the end, you will have gotten exactly what you want out of life, then the struggles and challenges you face in the meantime don't have to be such a big deal to you.

To get the most out of life—to have the best experience on this planet that you can have—you should take the attitude that you already know how it ends. You skipped to the last chapter of the book, and you found out that you came out on top; you saved the day, rescued the damsel in distress, got the castle and the crown—however you want to think of it. You won—whatever that means for you.

Now, you're free to enjoy the adventure that happens in between now and that time. You can look at your circumstances as all working together to help you become everything you want to be, and to accomplish and experience everything you want to accomplish and experience during the years between now and when you leave this planet.

This approach can really help you to stop and smell the roses, so to speak. Instead of looking at every little thing that comes up as something that is getting in the way of your success, you can look at these as things that can actually help you to get where you're trying to go; or at the very least, the things that make your adventure a more interesting story.

After all, the football games I've watched that were the most exciting, interesting, and satisfying were not the games where one team just kills the other one throughout the entire game. That actually gets boring. The games that are the most fun to watch, for me anyway, are the games where the victorious team has to beat and claw its way through challenges and setbacks in order to ultimately come out on top.

In fact, that's actually one of the reasons I enjoy watching football. I like watching the attitude of a winner who refuses to be discouraged in the face of adversity. I remember a couple of specific games where the winners were very impressive. Athletic ability aside, what really impressed me was the determination I saw in them—the attitude of a real winner. It appeared to me that they never doubted their ability to come back and win the game. Whether they actually had doubts or not, I really don't know. But it certainly didn't appear as though.

I can think of one game in the past several years where the University of Texas at Austin won the national championship (Hook 'em Horns!). They were down with only seconds to go in the game. It looked as if they were going to lose. I watched Vince Young in those last seconds to see how he was going to handle the situation. To me, it looked as if he had absolutely no doubt that he was going to win that game—and he did. In the last few seconds of the game, he made a very impressive drive then one final, amazing play to win the game and the championship. I could not see any discouragement in that player whatsoever—only determination and belief that he was going to win.

That's exactly how we need to be about being winners in our lives. We need to see our game as already won. Everything that happens between now and the end of our game will help us to be victorious, and will make the game interesting and more satisfying after we've won. We write our own story, so we know how it ends. And since we know how it ends, we can give ourselves permission to enjoy every chapter we have left until it ends.

Remember that our thoughts move our lives. If we want to move our lives to a higher level than 99.99 percent of the rest of the world, we need to use our thoughts to achieve that. Knowing in advance that in the end we are victorious, we can take the pressure off every little thing that happens to us in the meantime. We don't have to take every single setback or challenge so seriously. We can enjoy the ride.

Remember the saying I put up on my kitchen wall, "Today, I will think only positive thoughts; because if I think of only positive things today, I will be happy today, and my happiness will attract more positive things into my life."

If you know in advance that when your game is over, you come out the winner, it will be easier to maintain the right attitude during the process or during your "adventure." If you maintain the right attitude during your adventure, not only will you be able to enjoy the adventure more due to your improved attitude, but your more positive thoughts will actually change your adventure to be a more positive one because you will attract more positive experiences and results into your life. These improved results will help to ensure that you are, in fact, the winner when your game is over.

The other point I want to make in this section is to live *your own* adventure. Enjoy your own specific set of circumstances. Don't be envious of other people and their adventures—live your own adventure. It's easy to find someone to be envious of – there's always someone whose life seems more glamorous or fulfilling than yours, at least on the surface. But that only reinforces the feeling of lack, which results in more lack.

We don't know that someone else's adventure is going to be better than ours in the end. And if it is—so what? We only have our own adventure to live—let's make it the best it can possibly be. I have a feeling that if we learn how to do this adventure right, we'll look back without any desire whatsoever to trade places with anyone else.

Bonus Time

Here's an interesting concept that can sometimes help a person to relax a little bit and not worry so much about all the stressors in life.

Many of us can think back and remember a specific occasion when we narrowly escaped death; or perhaps even a time in our past when we thought we might be better off if we had moved on to the next phase of our existence.

If we can identify a specific event—or even a general timeframe—and look at all of our time after that as a bonus, we might feel more free to pursue the life we want without being so held back by fear.

There is more than one incident that I can think of. One that comes to mind for me is a time when I was living in Florianopolis, Brazil. This is still one of my favorite places in the world, but they do drive a little crazier down there than you're probably used to.

One day, I stepped off the curb behind a tall vehicle that I could not see around, and was attempting to cross the street. I was about to clear the vehicle when, at that exact moment, a very large bus came barreling right past my face at what seemed to be about one hundred miles per hour. I think it missed taking me with it against my will by about an inch and a half. If my timing had been off by half a second, I would have been splattered all over the front of that bus.

I could easily tell myself, *That's it—I should have been dead—now every moment I get after that almost-splat incident is a bonus. What do I want to do with my bonus?*

Can you picture yourself living without fear, knowing that you're living on your bonus time anyway? Whatever is holding you back from being, doing, and having what you want in life—can you let it go, knowing that it's all extra time anyway?

If you need to take this one step further to really grasp the attitude I'm trying to describe to you, how about this? What if you were to die today—but you got a chance to come back tomorrow? Everything past today is extra. It's all a big bonus—extra time that you can do whatever you want with. How would you spend that time? What would you do differently than before?

To illustrate it a different way—and this may strike a more familiar chord with some of you—you know what you do with your money every month, right? Yes, you pay your bills and meet your monthly living expenses—not too exciting, right?

Well, imagine that someone came along and said, "Okay—you've paid all your bills for the month. Now here's an extra $10,000 to be used for whatever will make you happy." This is not bill money, and it is not needed for any routine expenses. It's just for fun.

Would you enjoy that $10,000 more than the last $10,000 you earned? I'll bet you would. The last $10,000 you earned just went to obligations. This $10,000 is going to whatever you decide you'd like to spend it on.

We can do the same thing with the rest of our time here if we imagine it that way. If our "normal" life had ended at any of the points in the past where it easily could have—and we imagine everything after that point as a bonus—how much fun can we have with this extra time?

Do you think that if you keep this in mind you'll be better able to live without fear and just do what you really want to do in life? This idea may not be for everyone, but if it resonates with you, use it.

Scriptures on Faith

For those of you who like the Bible, here are just a few references on faith. When thinking about specific positive thoughts to have prepared in advance for whenever you're tempted to dwell on a negative thought, Bible verses can be very effective. These are just a few of the good ones for quick reference:

> Matthew 8:13: "Go! It will be done just as you believed it would."

> Matthew 9:22: "Your faith has healed you."

> Matthew 9:29: "It will happen to you just as you believed."

> Matthew 17:20: "If you have faith as small as a mustard seed, it is enough. You can say to this mountain, 'Move from here to there.' And it will move. Nothing will be impossible for you."

> Matthew 21:22: "If you believe, you will receive what you ask for when you pray."

Mark 9:23: "Everything is possible for the one who believes."

Mark 11:24: "…when you pray for something, believe that you have already received it. Then it will be yours."

Luke 8:48: "…your faith has healed you."

Luke 8:50: "…Don't be afraid. Just believe. She will be healed."

Luke 17:6: "Suppose you have faith as small as a mustard seed. Then you can say to this mulberry tree, 'Be pulled up. Be planted in the sea.' And it will obey you."

Luke 18:42: "Receive your sight. Your faith has healed you."

The Difference between Winners and Losers

In order to help you change your thinking from that of a loser to that of a winner, it may be helpful to point out some of the differences between the two mindsets. If you can remember these when a challenge arises, you can choose to respond to the situation as a winner would, instead of how a loser would. Here are just a few of the differences between winners and losers:

1. Losers dwell on problems; winners dwell on solutions.

2. Winners expect success; losers expect to fail.

3. Winners don't give up when things get difficult.

4. Winners focus on results, not excuses.

5. Winners don't try—they do.

6. Winners put in the extra effort when necessary.

7. Winners are self-confident, but not arrogant.

8. Winners think about how to turn negatives into positives.

9. Winners are comfortable in the presence of success and wealth.

10. Winners do not feel guilty for being successful.

11. Winners invest in themselves.

12. Winners are open to new ideas and they enjoy continuing to learn.

13. Winners realize that they don't know everything. They believe in the power of synergy and draw on the expertise of others.

14. Winners don't need to put others down in order to feel good about themselves.

15. Winners celebrate their successes and the successes of others.

16. Winners enjoy being successful, and enjoy helping others to become successful as well.

Feel free to add to this list—there are many other possibilities.

Defy Gravity

I'm going to define gravity, for our purposes, as the natural tendency for thoughts to become negative instead of positive. Just like the gravity that pulls us toward the earth instead of letting us float around in the air, the gravity of thought makes it so that if we're not actively doing something to keep our thoughts positive, they will tend to settle into the lower regions and become more negative.

Mental laziness allows this type of gravity to work. We get busy and don't even realize that we have stepped off of our "thinking program." We forget to read, listen, etc. to whatever positive programming we decided to keep putting into our minds, and instead, we get caught up in the "bad news" and we forget to mute all those horrible medication commercials on TV.

Can you imagine the "possible side effects" of watching hours and hours of medication commercials on TV? You'd probably get sick just because of all the negative images those commercials can put into your mind. And how about the music on those anti-depressant commercials? It seems like they're trying to make you depressed just so you'll buy their anti-depressants!

Stay away from negative thinking—don't let the high volume of bad health input cause you to get comfortable with the idea that everyone needs to be sick and taking a bunch of drugs all the time. Think health, happiness, love, and success!

Put forth the effort to continuously have positive input going into your brain. The moment you let up on this, the negative stuff will sneak in and try to take over. All you have to do is watch an hour of TV to see that this is true. Defy gravity in your thoughts—and your life will follow.

Scarcity and Competition

The field of economics deals with the allocation of "scarce" resources. This assumes that there is not enough to go around, and we must decide who gets what by some means or another.

I prefer to think *abundance* as opposed to *scarcity*. I prefer to think of limitations as being self-imposed and unnecessary as opposed to real. However, there are exceptions, and it's good to be aware of reality.

The fact is, most limitations are self-imposed, and, in reality, most people never realize their potential because they don't know how far they're actually capable of going.

There are some realistic limitations, and it's good to recognize them so that we can avoid unrealistic pipe-dreams and spend our time wisely and productively.

I will never be a professional basketball player. I am five feet, ten inches tall with shoes on, and recently celebrated my forty-ninth birthday. I accept these as real limitations for this specific objective, so I'm not going to waste my time working towards becoming a pro basketball player.

Of course, if I simply wanted to become a very impressive basketball player for my size and age, I absolutely believe that I could do that—if that were more important to me than certain other things are.

But the fact is, professional basketball is a very competitive area. There are a large number of people competing for a very small number of positions, and many of those people have advantages in that area that I will never have.

There are a number of areas like this that may be very difficult for certain people to make their mark in, simply because other people have an advantage over them in addition to also possessing the talent, drive, etc.

Again, I do believe that most limitations are self-imposed. But when you're dealing with positions that are highly desirable and very scarce, you need to assess where your natural advantages lie. What are your strengths and weaknesses? What are your talents? What are your interests?

Thinking abundance instead of scarcity, there are a number of areas where you can excel and perhaps become world class. Don't let others place unnecessary limitations on you. But do think to yourself, *Where can I best invest my time and other resources, maximizing my chances for success and happiness?*

Even though you can become good at whatever you want with enough effort, can you become better than others trying to do the same thing? Are you considering an area that is very difficult to enter or to become successful at because there are others with advantages that you will never have?

What areas do you have advantages in? Do you have a strong interest in, a talent for, a desirable physical attribute for, or another advantage in an area that you would like to pursue?

This is the idea behind the concept of "play to your strengths." If there are a number of possibilities and there is tough competition in many of them, maybe you should choose something you have a higher probability of succeeding at, as opposed to choosing something where your strengths do not lie but where others' strengths give them an advantage over you.

Of course, I cannot tell you what to choose, and if you have a strong passion for something, you may defy the odds and become better at it than someone else with more apparent advantages. That is certainly the application of not imposing limitations upon yourself.

I would say that most things will not carry this limitation, so I don't want to overstate this. A few areas do have extreme competition and there may be some realistic limitations. But I believe that most things are pretty wide-open for anyone who has the desire. And if you program your mind properly, success is almost guaranteed. If you avoid one of the extremely competitive areas where certain advantages that you may not possess are a pre-requisite to success, you can find a multitude of areas where you don't have to think about scarcity—you can focus on abundance.

In this world, you can climb as high as you want to go. You're creating what you want and there are no limits. You're not fighting a million other people for one carrot; you can grow as many carrots as you like.

Most of us will fall into this category of being able to focus on abundance instead of scarcity with what we do for a living. Instead of feeling like there's not enough to go around, I suggest visualizing an abundance of what you want—all yours for the taking. If you're in sales, visualize a huge group of people lined up and waiting to be helped by you. Don't worry about your "competition." Visualize an unlimited number of customers waiting in line to be helped by *you*.

I did this, and my business became just that. I was unable to help everyone who wanted my help. I simply did not have enough hours in the day. My main challenge became how to help all these people, not where customers were going to come from.

The main point that I'm trying to make here is that, unless your business is the exception to the rule and there are realistic limitations you have to be aware of and deal with appropriately, don't look at your business opportunities as being scarce. Have an attitude of abundance. You have the ability to create whatever you want in life—you don't have to compete with someone else over something that they want. What you want is in unlimited supply and no one is going to take it away from you.

Don't Do Your Best

Many of us were taught when we were children that it's okay to fail as long as we "do our best." And perhaps that's the right approach for children. But as adults, it's important to know what the phrases, "try" and "do your best" really mean when translated into the language of the subconscious mind.

I've actually seen adults set goals to "do their best," still hanging on to the belief that if you do your best, that's the most anyone can possibly expect of you. But there's a major problem with that way of thinking—it causes you to fail.

When it comes to how the subconscious mind deals with these commands, "try" and "do your best" are basically synonymous. They both tell the subconscious that its objective is not a specific result; it is simply an effort—and that failure is an acceptable result, as long as some effort has been made.

The fact is, if you're attempting something challenging, it's easier to fall short than it is to succeed. Succeeding generally requires more than failing does. All it takes to fail at something is to do one thing less than is required to succeed.

So, if the command we give our subconscious minds is not to succeed at something but merely to "try," the subconscious, which is a very efficient machine, will not do all that is required to succeed—it will do only what is required to show that some effort was made in that direction. It will stop short of what is required for success. In other words, it will intentionally fail.

But what about trying "your best?" Wouldn't that result in success, as long as success at that thing is possible for the person making the attempt? No. Again, the subconscious is an efficient, goal-seeking device. It will carry out what it perceives its orders to be. If we give it an order to "try" or to "do your best," the order is not to succeed—the order is not to produce a given result—the order is simply to make an attempt—and a failed attempt will do nicely. After all, a failed attempt is easier to produce than a successful attempt, and is therefore, a more efficient action.

So, do not program your subconscious mind to "try" or to "do your best," unless the result itself is unimportant to you. Program your mind to produce results. It is the result you're after—not the effort, right?

Change Your Physiology

Changing your physiology in advance is similar to the handwriting concept I mentioned earlier, in that the person can take what would normally be considered to be a result and use it as a cause. I might even suggest that the handwriting concept could be considered just one of many ways to use what is sometimes referred to as *the physiology of excellence*.

The concept is simple—that if you behave in certain specific ways, as if you already possess the traits you desire, these actions—normally considered to be results of the desired trait—can also help to cause the desired trait. This is due to the brain having already associated the desired trait with that specific physiology. It can also work with emotional states.

For example, a person smiles because he/she is happy. The smile is the result of feeling happy. But did you know that deliberately smiling when you do not feel happy may cause you to feel happier than you felt before you started smiling? In this way, the smile is used as the cause of feeling happy, not just a result of feeling happy. The two things are associated in the subconscious, and it doesn't necessarily matter which one comes first for the other one to also appear.

This concept puts you in the driver's seat—it gives you control over your emotional states, and can help program your subconscious mind to develop certain traits in you as well.

For example, let's say that you have decided you want to feel more confident in your professional setting. You work around assertive, confident people, and you believe that your lack of confidence has caused them to not respect you as much as you think they should.

Okay—so now let's make a list of every little thing you can think of that you might do a little differently if you were already more confident in that setting. Here are some things you could think about putting on that list:

- How would you dress if you were super confident?

- Would you use a different cologne or start using cologne?

- Would you walk differently?

- How would your voice change?

- How would the words you use change?

- When you shake someone's hand, would your handshake be a little firmer?

- When you are having a conversation with a co-worker or boss, would you look them in the eye a little more? Would you smile while looking them right in the eye and offering them a firm handshake, instead of waiting to see if they extend their hand while you nervously look back and forth?

- Would you stand up straighter?

- How would your posture be different than it is now?

- Would you pay more attention to your breath?

- Would you wear your hair differently or take better care of its appearance?

- Would you shine your shoes more often?

- Would you wash your car more often and make sure it's clean inside?

- Would you trim your fingernails more often?

- Would you speak to more people in the office or in a social situation than you do now?

- Would your response to conflict be more assertive than it is now? Could you smile and deal with a situation confidently yet assertively, rather than getting nervous and letting repressed emotions come out in a counterproductive way?

- Would you be more sociable at lunchtime or after work?

- Would you walk up to your boss with a suggestion instead of worrying that he/she might get irritated or that it might be a bad time?

- Would you handle criticism differently than you do now?

- Would your handwriting look different than it usually does?
- Would you decorate your office differently?
- Would you breathe differently?
- Would you exercise more than you do now?
- Would you eat differently?
- Would you spend your free time doing the same things you do now?
- Would you stand up and speak in public?
- Would you be more likely to sing Karaoke?

There are many more examples that could be listed here, and not all of these actually have to do with your personal physiology. But they all have to do with the same mindset. You can take things that are usually regarded as results of your desired trait and use these things as a cause—to program your subconscious mind that this trait you are manifesting through your actions is, indeed, your required and normal state.

You can use this *physiology of excellence* concept to increase professional and social confidence, success, health, sports performance, stage presence, job performance, negotiating ability, popularity, networking, even studying and test-taking performance.

What can this concept do for you? Try it and see—you may be surprised at the results.

Release Destructive Emotions

Emotions affect your life much more than most people realize. They have a strong impact on your health, for example.

Very often, we let destructive emotions build up in us and this can cause some nasty side effects. So how do we get rid of them? Well, we can blow our stack whenever the pressure builds up too high. That's probably not the best idea, and it certainly isn't an attractive option for the victims of our explosions. What else?

Well, many people seem to think that if they repress their emotions, there won't be any negative effects—and they won't have to bother dealing with the issues either—great choice! Well, not really. This can cause serious health problems and other ill effects they won't even be aware of.

How about if we release them in a civilized manner and allow more productive emotions to take their place? Yeah—that sounds like the right idea.

In many of the hypnosis sessions I have conducted, I helped people to release their destructive emotions by having them visualize the emotions they associated with a specific event or situation, as being some kind of black smoke. I instructed them to mentally move the black smoke from their entire body into the hand that they were using to squeeze on a squeeze ball or other non-harmful object.

Then, when all of the black smoke was isolated in that hand, I had them move all the black smoke out of their hand and into the ball or other object they are squeezing. I then had them nod their head when they were ready to open their hand and let all those negative emotions completely leave their body and mind.

When they were ready, I told them to open their hand, letting the object fall to the floor, and allow all those destructive emotions to completely leave them and to imagine the black smoke—their emotions—floating off into the distance, never to return. Then I had them feel the great relief and relaxation associated with allowing all those repressed emotions to finally leave them.

When I brought them out of hypnosis, their countenance was so incredibly different that I can't even describe it. It was so obvious that I think anyone would be able to see that it looked like a great weight had been lifted from their shoulders. One client looked as if she had never felt so happy in her entire life.

Though the result I got as a hypnotherapist might be stronger, you can do this exercise on your own. Just find a quiet place where you won't be interrupted, relax, and go through the exercise. Feel the emotions that you associate with any particular thing, situation, etc. Then imagine those emotions as black smoke, and continue through the rest of the exercise. This one little tip alone should be worth many times the cost of this book. The stress relief you can get from this will improve your health for the rest of your life.

(If you want an even more powerful solution to the effects of negative emotions stemming from events in your past, I really like Time Line Therapy®. Though you will need to consult a trained, certified practitioner, this can change your life and should be worth much more than it costs. If you can't find a certified practitioner in your area, feel free to contact me personally.)

Be Happy Now

Happiness is a choice. There are always positive and negative things around us, affecting our lives. The one we choose to dwell upon is the one that will grow in proportion to the other one.

Like the quote I hung up on my kitchen wall, if we dwell upon positive things, we will be happy, and we will attract more positive things. If we dwell on negative things, we will be unhappy, and we will attract more negative things.

Many people think that their happiness depends on the right set of circumstances. In reality, your right set of circumstances depends on your happiness. If you want to see what results you are creating for your life right now, examine your emotions regarding any specific issue. If they are consistently positive (happy), you are probably heading in a positive direction. If they are consistently negative (unhappy), you are most likely heading in a negative direction.

This is consistent with the feeling of either lack or the satisfaction of having already received what you desire. The feeling of lack attracts lack into your life. The feeling of enjoying already having what you desire attracts that thing or circumstance into your life. The manifestation of these results reveals whether your subconscious programming is productive or destructive.

And another thing: happiness and fulfillment in life is really the main goal anyway, right? So, why not get the added benefit of enjoying it earlier in life instead of later—or never?

If you postpone your happiness until you have the circumstances you think you need in order to be happy, you're continuously pushing those circumstances—and your happiness—into the future. And that future never comes, because there are always negative things to dwell upon— especially if you create more of them by focusing on the negative instead of the positive things that surround you.

The attitude of "happy now" attracts positive circumstances into your life. And that makes it easier to be happy—which attracts more positive circumstances— which results in a good life.

To start this positive cycle and be happy now, reprogram your mind using the steps in this book, and pay much more attention to the positive things in your life than to the negative things.

Don't expect all the negative stuff to just go away—just dwell on the positive stuff and start the cycle. You'll be setting yourself up for a happy life instead of a frustrating, miserable existence.

Remember—happiness is primarily the cause, not the effect. Don't wait for circumstances to change before you allow yourself to be happy. Change your circumstances by learning how to be happy first.

Everything everybody in the world wants is really with the end goal of their personal happiness and fulfillment. Money, success, health, love, possessions, respect—we want these things because we believe these things will make us happy. But if we wait until we have all of these things to be happy, not only are we postponing our happiness unnecessarily, but we're also repelling the very things we want to attract.

Remember: Happy first. Conditions second.

Count Your Assets

This idea utilizes several other techniques or concepts that we've already been through, in an attempt to trick your mind into believing that you already have what you desire.

Let's start with a simple question—where is your money? You might say, "I have about a thousand dollars in checking, maybe two thousand dollars in savings, and there might be twenty thousand dollars in my 401(k)." Okay, where else do you have assets that you can assign a value to? Maybe you have equity in a home; maybe a coin collection, art, automobiles, or other valuables.

Maybe you have considerably more in assets than we're talking about here, but you still believe that your programming can improve. Good—this will help.

We're used to thinking of certain types of assets as having a quantifiable value, like bank and investment accounts and equity in our homes. But the goal of this exercise is for you to feel wealthy now. I want you to be able to think to yourself, *I am a multi-millionaire right now!*

Instead of trying to believe something that is contrary to what you see, we can take an easier route. Allow me to show you that you already have some of these assets so that it will be easier to believe that you are in a certain position—so that it will be easier to attract more of what you want.

Let's count up some assets that you have not previously assigned a value to—but that realistically have value, at least to your future net worth. I want to use a little simple math to illustrate what I'm doing here.

Let's say that you have an income of $100/month that was left to you as part of an inheritance. This income is projected to continue indefinitely. If I were to ask you to count up your assets, you probably would not have thought to include this as an asset. But it is.

At the time I'm writing this, interest rates are very low. Money in the bank is paying almost nothing. It fluctuates of course, but let's say, for example, that a CD is paying 2 percent. To keep things simple, let's leave out interest earned month to month and just say that your $100/month is paid out to you as $1,200/year. How much principal would you have to have invested at 2 percent interest per year to generate an income of $1,200/year?

Here's the formula:

Interest Income / Interest Rate = Principal Required

In other words:

$1,200 / 2% = $60,000

See—that little $100/month income you didn't think to list as an asset can actually be assigned a value of $60,000!

Well, what other assets do you have that you have never thought of as having a quantifiable value? Yes, we are going to get creative here—that's part of the exercise.

How about your career? A supportive spouse? Good health? A good education? Future promotions that you can reasonably expect? Any intellectual property that may produce income in the future? Do you presently have any specific opportunities that you are reasonably convinced will produce a monthly income that you can put into the formula above?

What we're trying to do here is to count up some assets that you already have—and we want that number to be high—at least one million dollars. You can assign a value you believe to be reasonable to each asset you identify—but cap it at a maximum of 1,000,000 per asset.

These are things that you already possess, so when these assets are identified and a value is assigned to each of them—you can feel like you are a multi-millionaire right now! Yes, these assets may only pay off in the future—but a future cash flow has a present value!

So, for the sake of our example, let's say that you have identified five specific assets that you have assigned values to, totaling $2 million. You already have these assets, so you are now a multi-millionaire.

Next, we slip something in that you do not yet have. Let's say $100,000 in liquid savings. We justify this on the basis that once you put this goal into "the system" of believing before you receive, it's a done deal.

So now you use an affirmation, combined with the attitude of gratitude and visualization that you already have all this, and include the one thing that you do not actually have yet.

So—we're expressing gratitude to God, the universe, or whatever you believe in, with the sincere feeling that we already possess these things—but we've slipped in something that we're still waiting to receive.

There—we're acknowledging already having—with a strong emotional component—but we're including something that we desire, as if we've already received it. This will boost your effectiveness at attracting the thing you desire, and help to reprogram your mind so that you can start thinking of yourself as a person of means—a success.

I won't go through my list here, but I have a list of "long-term assets" that I am currently in possession of, with an assigned value of $10 million. And I slip in with this list a certain amount of current liquid assets that I would like to acquire in the near future. When I do my mental exercise, I know that I already possess these assets—so my emotional state is one of already having instead of lacking. When I get to the end of my list and include the cash balance I desire, I have already set myself up to be mentally and emotionally in the position of having, not lacking.

I suggest trying this over time, and see if you start to attract what you desire more effectively due to the feeling of already having, instead of the feeling of lacking, something that you desire. You could get a whole new attitude—and bank balance.

What Does She Have That You Can't Get?

Many years ago, I heard a question that has stuck with me until today. It was in a business opportunity meeting with a network marketing company geared toward women.

The middle-aged, high-school dropout, single mom who had once been flat broke and didn't know what she was going to do, walked up and took the stage to address the audience. She was dressed to kill, complete with mink coat, and looked fabulous by anyone's definition.

She started talking about whether the average new distributor could become successful at their business, and she made reference to someone else who was even higher in the organization, who had apparently become somewhat of an icon to their group.

After praising the achievements of this superwoman, I love the question she posed to the audience, "What does she have that you can't get?"

What a great attitude! In this scenario and most others, the answer is an obvious "nothing!"

A few years back, I was sales manager for a luxury home development in one of the more expensive areas of my city. The president of the company had challenged me to increase production to what appeared to be an unrealistic level. My job was to train, motivate, and manage this relatively new sales force into becoming an unstoppable, highly skilled group of top producers.

I decided to create a series of training sessions that would do just that. In the first part of our initial training session, after telling the group exactly what was being expected of us, I asked them, "Do you believe that there is a group of sales people anywhere in the world that is capable of achieving this goal?"

They responded that they did, indeed, believe that there must be a group of sales people somewhere in the world that possesses the skills necessary to achieve this task.

I then responded, "So—you do believe that this is possible? Someone on this planet is capable of doing this, right?" They responded, "Yes."

You can guess my next question, "What do they have that you can't get?" Of course, this made them think. Then we talked about the skills necessary to become top sales people. We broke this skill set down into defined categories and agreed that these skills are learnable. This gave the group confidence that they could become a highly skilled sales force capable of meeting this challenge.

It can be a good idea to find out who has what you lack and find out how they got it. They were most likely not born with it, and were certainly not born with it in a highly developed state.

Most qualities and skills can be learned, and thanks to the internet, information is very easy to find these days. If you set out to study successful people and understand how they became successful, you will see that the positive traits they possess are probably obtainable by the likes of you.

You may also notice that people who are highly successful in life do things differently than people who are not. Don't be surprised at this. If you want results that are different than what average people get, you have to do things differently than average people do them.

For You Analytical Types

(This is an optional section, designed for those who prefer a more detailed approach.)

Okay—let's talk more about taking action. After all, everything that's not action is preparation for action, right? First, your brain has to be programmed to help you to take the right actions instead of trying to prevent you from taking the right actions and causing you to take the wrong ones. Then, you have to have the attitudes, wisdom and motivation to take the right action. Then you have to get off your butt and do it! So let's go!

Action Plan

Here is an action plan that you can use to make sure you're maximizing your potential and getting the results you want.

Step #1: Divide *success* into the following classifications. I did this differently earlier, using only *be, do,* and *have.* But for those of you who prefer more details, let's use these seven categories:

1. Health

2. Marriage/Family/Relationships

3. Financial Status

4. Spirituality

5. Education (Knowledge/Wisdom)

6. Career/Business Success

7. Personal Goals

Step #2: Every calendar year or birthday, write in detail what you will do for each group.

A. Divide into sub-groups as appropriate

B. Use "N/A" and/or "Other" as appropriate

C. Be very realistic as to not let any one group create an over-load, for purposes of maintaining some degree of balance. Don't be so ambitious that the tasks won't get done.

D. Write down all the things you want to do, hope to do, wish you could do, etc. in each of the 7 (or more if you choose) categories.

E. Divide into groups to streamline and focus. Fewer things = more success, faster success or higher probability of success per thing. After writing down all the things you want to, hope to, or wish you could achieve, label them and put them into groups. Here are suggested groups:

i. Absolutely decided and committed to perform

ii. Want to perform, but can wait until a more important or more urgent goal is reached

iii. Can cancel or postpone indefinitely in order to increase the probability of success for other, more important items.

Make sure that you haven't put too much into the "absolutely committed to do" category for any of the seven subdivisions of *success*. You will probably have to go back and look at everything you wrote in all these categories and re-classify some things in order to get any real effectiveness in any single thing.

Once you have your goals categorized appropriately, break down, as best you can imagine, each goal into a sequence of actions that you believe will result in the achievement of that goal. If the goal is ongoing, list the set of actions you will need to take on an ongoing basis to maintain successful status in that area. Update your goals and/or action steps any time that something changes.

Keep in mind that as you reprogram your subconscious mind for success, it will reveal to your conscious mind better actions to take. So, you have to be flexible with the actions you list initially. Remember that when your programming is wrong, some of the actions you choose will be wrong as well.

When you improve your programming, your subconscious will set out to help you achieve your goals—instead of trying to prevent you from achieving them. One of the ways your subconscious mind will do this is to start giving you good ideas instead of bad ideas. Be flexible enough to incorporate better ideas when they come to you.

Step #3: Do end-of-year, quarterly and even monthly reports, as you choose. Plan for the next year, keeping records of past progress.

No matter what your approach is, it is a good idea to keep some kind of record of the goals you set out to achieve and were then successful in achieving. When you can look back on the successes you had using the process outlined in this book, it will be easier for you to believe in and achieve more and greater things.

Here is the goal achievement process again, this time divided into ten steps for the analytically inclined:

1.   Decide specifically and exactly what you want to be, do, or have—your objective. Do this separately for each of the seven categories above.

2.   Decide on the best external input to assist your thoughts in pointing you in that direction. Do your best to control your external input and dwell on these positive thoughts about accomplishing your objective, emphasizing the thought that your objective is already realized.

3.   Speak words out loud confirming that you have already accomplished your objective. Draft your phrases carefully, making sure to phrase them in the positive, the

present, and preferably with a positive emotion attached. Here's an example of a very short and sweet affirmation: "I enjoy making twenty thousand dollars a month."

4.   Picture in your mind that your objective is now realized. Visualize that you already are, are doing, or have what you desire. Construct in your mind short video clips that can be replayed as often as you like.

5.   Create and experience all the emotions related to now being, doing, or having what you set out to be, do, or have. Spend quiet time dwelling on the emotions you would feel if your objective were now realized. Properly release any conflicting emotions that may come up as you do this exercise.

6.   Express gratitude for having already realized your goal, as well as gratitude for the other positive things in your life, and all the challenges that can and are being turned into positive things. Remember that everything that happens to you can be turned into a positive in some way.

Focus on the positive results—dwell on the solution, not the problem, and maintain an attitude of gratitude that the problem has already been turned into the solution; the negative has already been turned into a positive, if applicable in this case.

7.   Set out to gain all necessary wisdom as to what you can do to obtain your objective. Write out a plan, breaking down the actions necessary into small and manageable steps that you believe would result in the realization of your goal.

8. Take any associated actions required to fulfill the objective, following and revising as necessary the steps written in item #7, above. Make sure to be receptive to new ideas that may come up from your subconscious mind as your positive reprogramming starts to replace the negative programming from your past.

9. Any time that any conflicting thoughts, words, mental pictures, emotions, external input or lack of gratitude attempts to enter your mind, have something prepared and ready to replace the negative stimulus and execute the switch immediately and forcefully (and maybe even with a little drama).

10. Repeat steps 2-9 until the goal is realized. Remember to not take on too many goals at once. You don't have to achieve all your goals in the first month or year. Focus on what's most important—get some goals achieved; then move on to bigger and better goals gradually as you become more expert at using this system.

Make sure to keep some kind of balance in your life. Don't over-emphasize one area to the point that another important area is ignored. Yes, you do have to focus and not spread yourself too thin, but something resembling a proper balance is still going to have to occur in order to have a happy life long term.

Endnotes

Winners win and losers lose. You can tell whether you are a winner or a loser by your long-term results. You may have all the great qualities that should be required to be a winner, but your long-term results are conclusive. That's why I said earlier that I used to be a loser. My long-term results were conclusive. Sure, I had a bunch of positive qualities and a lot of potential, but my results revealed my programming. From my results, it was clear that I needed to reprogram my subconscious mind.

Even though I thought of myself as a positive thinker who believed that anything is possible, I found myself in my forties—broke, with no real career, twice divorced, with heath problems, having accomplished only a small fraction of what I intended to accomplish by this time. Worst of all, I was unhappy and frustrated with life. After discovering what went wrong and how to fix it, I am now still in my forties, deliriously happily married, miraculously healthy, with a real career, making lots more money than I was a short time ago, and actually starting to accomplish my goals. Most importantly, I am finally happy and I truly believe that things are only going to continue to improve.

Yes, this stuff really works. And I put the formula in this book so that you can benefit from it as well.

How about you? Are you a loser? If your results suggest so, then you probably are. Now, don't go getting all depressed over it. This is great news, indeed! Once a diagnosis is made, a solution can be identified—a plan of action can be custom-written for you, to make sure you overcome this problem. And this plan does not include wallowing in your loser-ness. Decide now to leave that loser-ness behind you and become a winner. Decide now that it is time to not waste another second of your life being a failure—you can become a success, you just needed to find out what was wrong and how to fix it.

What determines whether you are successful or not is really up to you. If you are happy with where you are in life, who you are, what you do, your financial condition, etc., then you are a success by your own definition and that's what's important.

If you are frustrated in life, have financial troubles, or are experiencing failure in your relationships or your health due to financial difficulties or frustration about the state of your life, then it's difficult to be happy or to see yourself as a winner.

Success, of course, is not just about material things. To me, success includes things like what kind of person you are. Do you have a set of beliefs that you live by? Your religious or spiritual beliefs would apply here. Are you the person you believe that you should be? Are you missing something in this area?

Socrates said, "The unexamined life is not worth living." When you examine your life, do you feel that your life has meaning? Do you have a sense of fulfillment and purpose? If not, I would suggest making this one of your priorities.

Success also includes your education, career, other accomplishments, hobbies, and anything else you want to be and do with your life. Are you unhappy with your level of education? Should you consider going back to school full or part time?

How's your career? Are you holding back because of negative programming? Do you know you could do better or rise higher if you just applied yourself more?

Are there worthy but unfulfilled desires that you no longer believe are realistic? Maybe it's not too late. Remember the George Eliot quote—this is one of my favorites—"It's never too late to be what you might have been." Maybe it's not too late to accomplish some of the dreams you've given up on. Maybe there's still time to be satisfied with your life-adventure overall.

Maybe you just need to stop holding back and start applying the concepts in this book to your life and get some enthusiasm back into your thinking—to make your life the adventure it's supposed to be.

Success is being happy with the direction your life is headed and the speed it's heading there. If you can use the steps outlined in this book to stay focused on what you want and to create a strong magnetism between you and your goals, your life can change direction. When you point your life in the direction you want to go in, then continuing to use these concepts will help you to speed up the process, and you'll get what you want out of life even faster.

When you can see the results of your becoming what you want to be, doing what you want to do, and having what you want to have, you are now a success—a winner. You have risen above your previous loser status.

Let's not forget about finances, of course. That's what most people think of when they hear the word *success*. I don't believe that a person who becomes rich at the expense of more important things is truly successful. But I do believe it is possible to have it all.

And for me personally, I accept it as my responsibility to have enough to live and provide a life for my wife that is free of financial stress, that leaves no regrets—no important goals in life unachieved, and that places no financial burden on anyone else. That is my personal view of financial success. I believe in living life to the fullest—and that costs money.

Remember that we shouldn't always pre-judge when something happens whether it is good or bad. Keep the attitude that it's either good or can be made good. Before I really got serious about writing this book, I had a day that could have been really rotten. I had to go into the office, simply to pick up the power cord to my laptop that I had forgotten the night before. I didn't have time, but I really needed it. So I got in the car—just to find the worst traffic I'd ever seen getting to my office. It took me around ninety minutes to get to my office, and I only lived a few minutes away. Most of the time I was just sitting there burning gas.

Fortunately, when I started getting frustrated with the situation, I decided to recite in my mind *Rico's Rules for Dealing with Challenges*. When I got to "Every negative can be turned into a positive," I decided to turn this situation into something positive. I wanted to make sure that I turned it around so well that I would actually be happy that I had to sit in traffic for so long.

Imagine that, huh? Well, it worked! I wound up getting some good ideas that I incorporated into this book— and I was actually able to write them down in the car because traffic was so stopped up. Here's a sample of my notes from that morning in the car:

> Deciding what you want to be/do/have can be the most difficult and most critical part. If you're having trouble with this, start with one thing and leave the rest open for the time being. Just don't give into indecision and confusion, which stops the process of getting what you want. And trying to work on or attract too many different things at once dilutes your effectiveness. You *must* have a clear vision of what you want. Make sure it is clearly defined.

After these thoughts came to my mind, while still stuck in traffic, I decided that my first "decide and focus" objective would be to finish this book and get it published. I had started on it a little while back, but I had gotten so busy that I really hadn't done anything with it for a while. During this traffic incident, I not only got some insights that I wanted to incorporate into the book, but I also made the decision to make it a priority to actually get it finished and published.

Here's another sample I found that I believe may have come from my car notes during the traffic incident:

> Instead of just trying to attract something to you, what you really want to do is to create a strong magnetism between you and the thing you desire. Instead of just expecting the thing to move toward you, you can also move toward it. This allows for action on your part. Though you may not start out knowing the appropriate action to take, as you program this magnetism into your subconscious, the best actions to take will become apparent to you; then you have to allow yourself to take those actions.
>
> When you're visualizing having what you want, maybe try also visualizing yourself taking actions—allow your subconscious to show you what actions you should take. Then allow yourself to take those actions. This way, you are attracting what you desire to you—but also attracting yourself to what you desire. In other words, you're creating a strong magnetism between you and what you desire, causing both yourself and what you desire to move toward each other.

As you can see, by using one of the concepts I wrote about, not only did I get some insights that I was able to include in the book, but it was actually that moment of turning a negative into a positive that helped me to solidify my goal of actually getting this book done. I am now thankful that this "negative" occurred. Without it, I don't know if this book would have ever been published. Other good things have also happened in my life as a domino effect of this single "negative" event because I chose to turn it into a positive.

Well, I think I've said what I intended to, so I guess it's time to wrap up. If you want to change your life, now you have a way to make it happen. Remember—results, not excuses. Focus on results, and get results. Don't make excuses as to why you couldn't do it—program your mind to allow you and to help you to do it. When your 88 percent starts to *want* what your 12 percent wants, your results will be far greater than you've experienced in the past, and your life can become richer, fuller, and happier than you ever imagined.

Here's to your success!

Epilogue

In conclusion, I would like to leave you with one of my favorite quotes. This is from our twenty-sixth American president, Theodore Roosevelt:

> It is not the critic who counts; not the man who points out how the strong man stumbles, or where the doer of deeds could have done them better. The credit belongs to the man who is actually in the arena, whose face is marred by dust and sweat and blood, who strives valiantly; who errs and comes short again and again; because there is not effort without error and shortcomings, but who does actually strive to do the deed; who knows the great enthusiasm, the great devotion, who spends himself in a worthy cause, who at the best knows in the end the triumph of high achievement and who at the worst, if he fails, at least he fails while daring greatly. So that his place shall never be with those cold and timid souls who know neither victory nor defeat.

We have one shot at this life, my friends. It is my sincere desire that every one of you reading this book will find the inspiration, motivation, and belief necessary to do whatever it takes to become all that you can be—so that in the end, we may all be able to look back on our lives with great satisfaction, having no regrets but only immense joy from the time we were able to spend here on this exciting adventure we call our lives. God bless you throughout your journey.

listen|imagine|view|experience

AUDIO BOOK DOWNLOAD INCLUDED WITH THIS BOOK!

In your hands you hold a complete digital entertainment package. In addition to the paper version, you receive a free download of the audio version of this book. Simply use the code listed below when visiting our website. Once downloaded to your computer, you can listen to the book through your computer's speakers, burn it to an audio CD or save the file to your portable music device (such as Apple's popular iPod) and listen on the go!

How to get your free audio book digital download:

1. Visit www.tatepublishing.com and click on the eILIVE logo on the home page.
2. Enter the following coupon code:
   bbe9-2ade-9e1f-184b-3c43-5d7b-b2f5-0ebc
3. Download the audio book from your eILIVE digital locker and begin enjoying your new digital entertainment package today!